BUFFERING TECHNIQUES FOR DELIVERY OF COMPRESSED VIDEO IN VIDEO-ON-DEMAND SYSTEMS

THE KLUWER INTERNATIONAL SERIES IN ENGINEERING AND COMPUTER SCIENCE

MULTIMEDIA SYSTEMS AND APPLICATIONS

Consulting Editor

Borko Furht
Florida Atlantic University

Recently Published Titles:

HUMAN FACE RECOGNITION USING THIRD-ORDER SYNTHETIC NEURAL NETWORKS, by Okechukwu A. Uwechue, and Abhijit S. Pandya
ISBN: 0-7923-9957-9

MULTIMEDIA INFORMATION SYSTEMS, by Marios C. Angelides and Schahram Dustdar
ISBN: 0-7923-9915-3

MOTION ESTIMATION ALGORITHMS FOR VIDEO COMPRESSION, by Borko Furht, Joshua Greenberg and Raymond Westwater
ISBN: 0-7923-9793-2

VIDEO DATA COMPRESSION FOR MULTIMEDIA COMPUTING, edited by Hua Harry Li, Shan Sun, Haluk Derin
ISBN: 0-7923-9790-8

REAL-TIME VIDEO COMPRESSION: Techniques and Algorithms, by Raymond Westwater and Borko Furht
ISBN: 0-7923-9787-8

MULTIMEDIA DATABASE MANAGEMENT SYSTEMS, by B. Prabhakaran
ISBN: 0-7923-9784-3

MULTIMEDIA TOOLS AND APPLICATIONS, edited by Borko Furht
ISBN: 0-7923-9721-5

MULTIMEDIA SYSTEMS AND TECHNIQUES, edited by Borko Furht
ISBN: 0-7923-9683-9

VIDEO AND IMAGE PROCESSING IN MULTIMEDIA SYSTEMS, by Borko Furht, Stephen W. Smoliar, HongJiang Zhang
ISBN: 0-7923-9604-9

BUFFERING TECHNIQUES FOR DELIVERY OF COMPRESSED VIDEO IN VIDEO-ON-DEMAND SYSTEMS

by

Wu-chi Feng
The Ohio State University

SPRINGER SCIENCE+BUSINESS MEDIA, LLC

Library of Congress Cataloging-in-Publication Data

A C.I.P. Catalogue record for this book is available
from the Library of Congress.

ISBN 978-1-4757-7070-4 ISBN 978-0-585-31403-7 (eBook)
DOI 10.1007/978-0-585-31403-7

Originally published by Kluwer Academic Publishers in 1997
Softcover reprint of the hardcover 1st edition 1997

Printed on acid-free paper.

To my parents, Carol, and our newborn Ryan

CONTENTS

LIST OF FIGURES

LIST OF TABLES

PREFACE

As the year 2000 approaches, we are witnessing an explosive growth in networked multimedia services that are available. The World-Wide-Web (WWW) is exponentially growing in size and will continue to do so in the years to come. In conjunction with web browsers, the WWW allows for the retrieval of multimedia information including sound, images, and video. In addition to the WWW, many new services are becoming available such as Digital Satellite System (DSS) or High-Definition Television (HDTV) broadcasts, which have been promised within the next 10 years. One important key will be the efficient handling of digital video within these contexts.

In this monograph, we examine how to efficiently deliver stored video streams across networks for applications such as video-on-demand and digital libraries. The goal of this book is to provide an in-depth examination of buffering techniques for the delivery of constant quality, variable-bit-rate, stored video. We will examine techniques for *smoothing* the bandwidth requirements in the delivery of stored video and examine extensions that are required in order to provide interactive services to users. To highlight the various techniques that are presented in this book, we have captured a large library of full-length movies and show how these techniques apply to videos that may actually be transmitted in a video-on-demand implementation.

The book is organized into five main sections: 1) *Preliminaries*, covering basic video compression algorithm such as MPEG and Motion-JPEG; 2) *Bandwidth Smoothing Algorithms*, which formulates the problem of delivering stored video across networks and how buffering techniques can be used to smooth the bandwidth requirement from the underlying network and server; 3) *A Bandwidth Smoothing Survey*, comparing and contrasting several bandwidth smoothing algorithms that have appeared in the literature; 4) *Interactivity in Bandwidth Smoothing Environments*, describing a basic infrastructure that may be used to provide interactive video-on-demand services to users; and 5) *Bandwidth Smoothing for Interactivity*, which describes a new class of bandwidth smoothing algorithms more sensitive to the needs of interactive video-on-demand services. A more detailed description of the individual parts of the book may be found in Section 1.3.

Wu-chi Feng
The Ohio State University

wuchi@cis.ohio-state.edu
June 1997

1

INTRODUCTION

1.1 Background

Multimedia has a virtually unlimited number of applications that can significantly affect the lives of people. Applications such as world-wide-web (WWW) browsers (along with the web-servers they access) allow people to share information in a multimedia format that includes text, audio, still images, and to an extent, video. Live-video conferencing and computer supported collaborative work (CSCW) applications allow physically separated people to interactively discuss and share ideas through the exchange of multimedia information. Applications such as digital libraries and video-on-demand services promise the retrieval of video for virtually any topic the user desires. A common thread throughout all these applications is the need for high quality video within limited resource budgets.

The handling of digital video poses a formidable task to virtually any computer or network system. As an example, a one second 640x480 pixel video clip in 24-bit mode requires approximately 27.6 Megabytes (MBytes) of data to be handled in one second. Furthermore, to store a minute of this video in uncompressed format would require over 1.5 Gigabytes of data. To reduce the large resource requirements that these videos place on the underlying systems, video compression techniques such as the Motion Pictures Expert Group's (MPEG) compression standard or Motion-JPEG compression have been introduced. For constant quality compression, however, these standards result in bursty, variable bit rate video, making efficient resource allocation more difficult. For long video clips, this burstiness requires the delivery system to adjust to fluctuations in both long-term (> 10 minutes) and short-term (< 1 sec) bandwidth requirements.

1.2 Research Objectives

In this monograph, we take an in-depth look at how burstiness introduced by compression standards such as MPEG and Motion-JPEG affects the efficient delivery of video streams across networks. We concentrate on the handling of bursty prerecorded video data that may be found in an interactive educational system or an interactive video-on-demand video delivery system. Our two-fold approach focuses on techniques for the continuous delivery of video streams across networks and techniques for delivering video in interactive environments.

Video compression techniques can be applied to both live and stored video applications; however, the handling of the data for these two types of applications have vastly different requirements. Live video applications are typically constrained by the need for network bandwidth scheduling decisions to be made on-line and the delay between sender and receiver minimized. As a result, handling compressed live-video typically requires that statistical guarantees be made for both network and system resources or adjusting the picture quality to fit within a fixed size channel. On the other hand, stored video applications have different needs for network and system resources. Because the video is stored, the delay between sender and receiver does not necessarily need to be minimized as long as the data is received by the playback instance. Thus, buffering can be an effective tool for the handling of compressed prerecorded video data.

For the delivery of prerecorded video data, we introduce the notion of *critical bandwidth allocation*. This bandwidth smoothing technique creates a bandwidth allocation plan for the delivery of the video data given *a priori* knowledge of the video data. The critical bandwidth allocation technique allows for the retrieval of stored video that does not require any initial prefetching (and hence, delay) and results in a monotonically decreasing sequence of bandwidth allocations. Given some fixed buffer size constraint, the critical bandwidth allocation algorithm creates plans for the continuous playback of stored video that have (1) the minimal number of bandwidth increases, (2) the smallest peak bandwidth requirement, and (3) the largest minimum bandwidth requirement. We extend this idea into an *optimal bandwidth allocation policy* that, in addition to the critical bandwidth algorithm properties, also minimizes the total number of bandwidth changes required for the continuous playback of stored video.

While the use of bandwidth smoothing techniques are effective at removing the peak bandwidth requirements of networks for a single video stream, smoothing of bandwidth through the prefetching of data makes the bandwidth plans somewhat rigid. This, in turn, makes it difficult to support VCR capabilities such as stop, pause, rewind, and fast-forward. To support these interactive functions, we examine two techniques that can be used to aid in resource allocation of video-on-demand systems. First, we introduce the notion of the *VCR-window*, which allows users to have full-function VCR capabilities within a limited segment of video around the playback point without having to change the level of the bandwidth reservations. For accesses outside the VCR-window re-negotiation of network resource may be necessary. To allow for these accesses, we show how the use of a "contingency channel" for stored video can be used to resynchronize the delivery of video back with the original bandwidth allocation plan. To show the applicability of the VCR-window, we introduce a resource reservation scheme that can be used in conjunction with the VCR-window.

In addition to the VCR-window, we introduce several techniques for creating bandwidth allocation plans that are more amenable to interactive service. We introduce a *rate-constrained bandwidth smoothing* algorithm which, for a given rate constraint, minimizes the smoothing buffer required for playback of a video and also minimizes the smoothing buffer utilization. We extend the idea of the rate-constrained bandwidth smoothing algorithm into a *time-constrained bandwidth smoothing* algorithm and a *time/rate* constrained bandwidth smoothing algorithm. These algorithms allow for the delivery of video that have interactivity in mind but still provide the advantages that the *critical bandwidth* based smoothing algorithms offer.

1.3 Outline of the Monograph

The structure of the monograph is as follows. In Chapter 2, we present necessary background for the rest of the chapters. We begin by describing our assumptions about the structure of the video-on-demand system. We also describe the work that has been introduced for video servers and for video retrieval techniques. A discussion of compression technologies and how burstiness is introduced into video streams is presented. Finally, we conclude the chapter with a description of a video capture testbed that we used to capture over 30 GBytes of video data for use as sample clips in this dissertation.

Chapter 3 deals with the problem of delivering a single compressed prerecorded video stream across networks. Specifically, we describe two broad classifications of smoothing techniques: window-based and non-window-based smoothing techniques. We present two window-based techniques that smooth bandwidth requirements based on some maximum delay (window) that each frame must adhere to. We then present the *critical bandwidth allocation* algorithm and the *optimal bandwidth allocation* algorithm, which do not adhere to a window, allowing burstiness to be smoothed over larger stretches of video. Finally, we compare, contrast, and summarize the differences between the various algorithms.

Since the introduction of the *critical bandwidth allocation algorithm* and the *optimal bandwidth allocation algorithm* several other bandwidth smoothing techniques have been introduced in the literature. In Chapter 4, we present an in-depth comparison of the bandwidth smoothing algorithms that have been presented in the literature, highlighting the unique properties that each algorithm possesses.

In Chapter 5, we focus on the problem of handling multiple video streams. Specifically, we introduce the VCR-window and describe how burstiness affects the ability to provide VCR functionality. We then describe a contingency channel mechanism that can be used for accesses outside of the VCR-window, where renegotiation of network bandwidth may need to be done. To show how the VCR-window can be used, we describe an in-advance resource reservation scheme for scheduling network resources. Finally, we then use our sample video clips to show the effectiveness of the VCR-window and its affect on the underlying network manager.

Chapter 6 presents a class of bandwidth smoothing algorithms that are more amenable to providing VCR functions. We first present the *rate-constrained*, *time-constrained*, and *time/rate constrained* bandwidth smoothing algorithms and provide the intuition behind what each algorithm attempts to accomplish. We then compare and contrast these algorithms with the algorithms presented in Chapter3.

In Chapter 7, we review the contributions of this dissertation and summarize some of the key findings of this research. Finally, we present some future directions for research in these areas.

2

PRELIMINARIES

In this chapter, we present the necessary background for the remaining chapters of this dissertation. We describe the current trends in video-on-demand systems, highlighting the work on video-on-demand servers and network transportation protocols. In addition, we describe the relevant details of image and video compression necessary for the understanding of this dissertation.

2.1 Video Retrieval Systems

Video retrieval systems involve two separate layers: the timely retrieval of information from video-based file systems and the real-time transfer of the data to end users. In this section, a description of academic and industrial efforts aimed at providing real-time access to video file systems is given followed by a description of high level protocols that attempt to reserve bandwidth specifically for video data.

2.1.1 Video-On-Demand Architectures

Video-on-demand (VOD) systems that have been proposed in the literature typically consist of three main components: a large archive server, an intermediate cache server, and clients (Figure 2.1). Recent developments in file systems and disk systems such as RAIDs (Redundant Array of Inexpensive Disks) allow file systems to achieve greater throughputs, alleviating some potential bottlenecks in the file system. As a result, it is now possible for a single VOD server to handle many clients simultaneously.

Typically, one or more archive servers reside at the top of the VOD hierarchy. These servers typically have large tertiary storage devices, such as magnetic tape jukeboxes for mass storage of video at a relatively low cost [FEDE94]. To allow for efficient

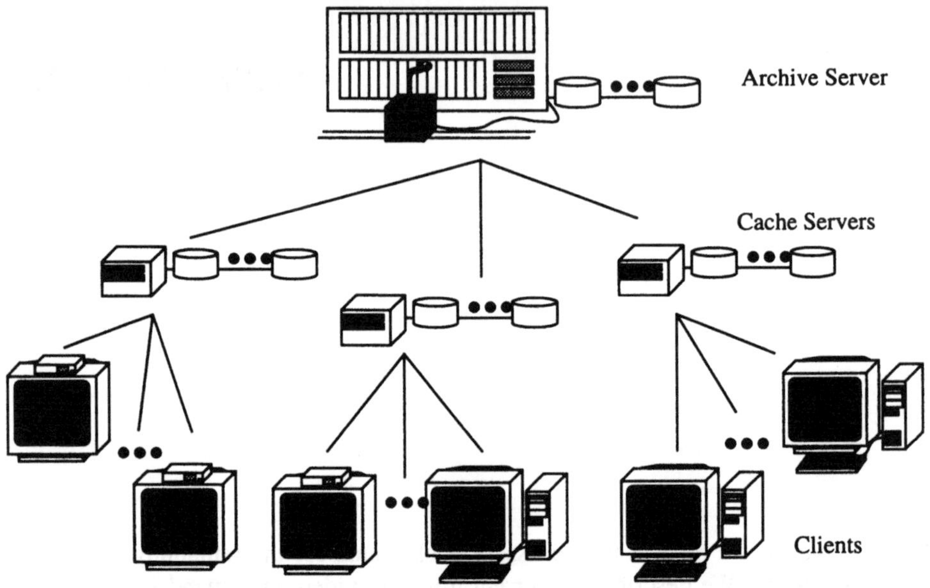

Figure 2.1: A Sample Video-On-Demand Architecture. This figure shows a sample hierarchical VOD architecture. The archive server typically consists of a large tertiary storage such as magnetic tape and large disks to hold entire movies. The cache servers act as load balancers for the more popular movies. Clients may consist of either workstations or set-top-boxes.

transport of video to the caching servers, the archive servers download the requested data on to large disks on the archive server. The requested data is then transferred in bulk to the cache servers.

A cache servers consists of several large disks (on the order of 50-100 GBytes) so that the more popular videos can be cached in their entirety [ANDE92, GEMM95, KAND94, LOUG93], distributing the load of access requests away from the archive servers. Video requests that are not present on the cache servers are requested from an archive server. Because the cache servers have enough buffering to hold on the order of 50-100 movies, the delivery of the video data from the archive server can be transferred in a large burst of bandwidth into the caching server's disk. We expect that a large portion of the video requests would be handled by the caching servers. One recent study suggests that the access frequencies for various movies can be modeled by a Zipf distribution model, and that only 38 movies cover more than 70% of all requests in a single week [DAN94]. Note that the set of clients that a caching server may service is not fixed. A client may choose one of a number of nearby servers, just as a customer at a video rental store may go to the next convenient store in the vicinity, if the client cannot find the title of the movie that they are looking for.

The clients within the VOD architecture consist of either desktop computers with support for digital video or a set-top-box devoted solely for viewing compressed video. We assume that clients have some buffering available (either disk or RAM) for smoothing of network bandwidth requirements, but in order to keep consumer costs down, we expect that these client boxes do not have large reserves of buffering available. We also assume that the clients contain enough intelligence to create bandwidth allocation plans and to interact with the network and servers. Because of these constraints, the transportation of video from the cache server to the clients must be monitored so that the clients are not over-run with data or starved of data. In addition, these interactions must be made such that the underlying link layer can be used as effectively as possible.

The network provides the pathway between the video servers and their clients. The only assumption we make about the network is that it can provide network resource guarantees based either on some rate-based or real-time channel approach [ARAS94, ZHAN91] and that the network provides some mechanism for in-advance reservations of bandwidth [DEGE95, FERR95, WOLF95]. The network resource guarantees are necessary to ensure a quality of service (QOS) level to the users. We assume that the bandwidth reserved on these channels will be delivered assuming the channel has already been admitted. Furthermore, we assume that the admission control and the reservations for network resources can be done in advance, making network scheduling and load estimation easier for the network [LITT94].

2.1.2 Video retrieval techniques

The delivery of data to a client can be handled in one of several ways. The simplest approach is to deliver the video in a best-effort fashion, resulting in no guarantees in QOS. As a result, packets may be arbitrarily delayed or dropped. Delivering high quality video in this environment has been studied in the literature [JEFF92]. At the other end of the spectrum, bandwidth can be reserved at the peak bandwidth requirement for the video. Allocating at the peak bandwidth requirements without bandwidth smoothing, however, results in very conservative estimates of the actual resources required. In between these extremes lies two other techniques, statistical multiplexing and bandwidth smoothing techniques.

Statistical multiplexing has been introduced to take advantage of the law of large numbers. This technique reserves bandwidth for a video channel very near to the mean of the video frame sizes expected [REIN93]. Then, during the delivery of data, each video stream transmits a frame of video every 1/30th of a second, where the various multiplexed streams approach the sum of all the averages. This method typically can deliver 95% or more of all packets provided that the channel can deliver a significant number of streams, but no guarantees on the delivery of a packet are given. Statistical multiplexing techniques are suitable for live-video applications, where frames are being digitized and transmitted in real-time. For stored video applications, the use of statistical multiplexing implies that the server must transmit one frame every 1/30th of a second. This, however, results in a large amount of burstiness that the server has to account for in its retrieval off of slower storage devices, leading to scalability problems.

Unlike statistical multiplexing schemes, bandwidth smoothing techniques attempt to remove the burstiness of the video by introducing delay so that the bandwidth requirements can be reduced. Bandwidth smoothing techniques require buffering to reduce the variance in necessary bandwidths. For video-on-demand systems, bandwidth smoothing techniques are useful because they do not require that the time between video capture and video playback to be minimized. As a result, resource allocation plans can be made before playback begins, resulting in channels that can have bandwidth guarantees. In addition, bandwidth smoothing techniques allow the load on the video servers to be smoothed, resulting in a more scalable design.

2.2 Compression Technologies

In order to reduce the sheer amount of data that is required to represent an image, compression technologies have been developed that have a compression ratio of roughly 25:1 for still images and 50-100:1 for video. The additional compression derives from dependencies between frames. In this section, we present a high-level description of the Joint Photographic Expert's Group (JPEG) image compression standard and the Motion Picture Expert's Group (MPEG) video compression standard. The JPEG standard, while originally aimed at still-images, forms the basis for the MPEG video compression standard and is therefore necessary for the understanding of the MPEG video standard. Following our discussion of JPEG, we then give a high-level description of the MPEG motion video compression standard in as much detail as necessary for the discussions in this dissertation.

2.2.1 JPEG Image Compression

The JPEG image compression standard is a "lossy" image compression technique that uses knowledge of visual perception of the human eye to allow for a relatively high compression ratio. We refer readers interested in the lower level details to the JPEG standard and its companion introductory paper [WALL91].

The JPEG compression standard comprises of four main steps (Figure 2.2). The compression algorithm operates on 16 pixel by 16 pixel squares called *minimum coding units* or *macroblocks*. For each macroblock, a conversion from the red, green, blue (RGB) color space into the *YUV* color space is performed. This transformation allows the more important luminance component (*Y*) to be separated from the two chromi-

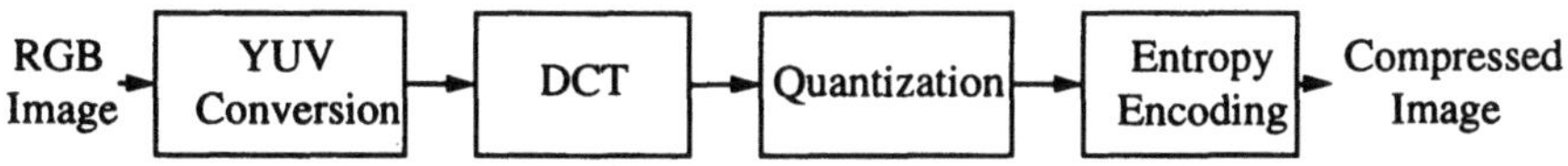

Figure 2.2: JPEG Overview. This figure shows the four main steps involved in compressing an image into the JPEG format. 1) Conversion of RGB color space to YUV color space, 2) Transformation into frequency domain via discrete cosine transform (DCT), 3) Quantization of DCT values, and 4) Entropy encoding (using either Huffman or arithmetic encoding).

nance channels *U* and *V*. The luminance component is essentially the brightness of each pixel. The human eye is most sensitive to small changes in the luminance component, while changes in the chrominance channels must be larger to be easily perceived by the human eye. Once the *YUV* transformation is complete, the luminance component is subdivided into four 8x8 pixel blocks, while the chrominance components are subsampled from two 16x16 pixels blocks into two 8x8 pixel blocks, one for the *U* channel and one for the *V* channel. As a result this step is somewhat "lossy" in the chrominance channels. Next, these six 8x8 blocks are compressed.

Compression in JPEG takes place in three steps: discrete cosine transformation (DCT), quantization, and entropy encoding. First, the DCT transforms each of the 8x8 pixel blocks into the frequency domain. This transformation moves the lower frequency components into the upper left corner of the block while moving the higher frequency components into the lower left corner. Thus, the average value (or DC level) of each block is in the upper left corner. The other 63 coefficients are called the AC values. In the second step, the coefficients are quantized into discrete levels giving coarser distinctions for higher frequency components. This is considered the "lossy" part of the compression standard. The JPEG standard allows for varying qualities by allowing the coarseness of the quantization matrix to be specified by the user. The more bits that are used in the quantization (and hence more levels), the closer the reconstructed picture is to the original. Finally, the run-length encoded coefficients for each block are compressed with either Huffman or arithmetic encoding. To retrieve the original image, the above process is reversed.

2.2.2 Motion-JPEG and MPEG Video Compression

In order to compress video streams, a natural extension of the JPEG still image standard is to apply it to a stream of successive images for video, resulting in a stream of JPEG compressed images (Motion-JPEG or MJPEG). While relatively simple, this compression technique does not take advantage of similarities between frames. Because of high frame to frame correlation, the similarities between frames can be used to achieve considerably higher compression rates. The MPEG video compression standard is a layered video compression standard that results in VHS quality

MPEG Layer	Function
Sequence Layer	Random Access Unit: context
Group of Pictures Layer	Random Access Unit: video
Picture Layer	Primary Coding Unit
Slice Layer	Resynchronization Unit (within picture)
Macroblock Layer	Motion Compensation Unit Within Slice
Block Layer	DCT Unit Within Macroblock

Table 2.1: The MPEG Video Compression Layers.

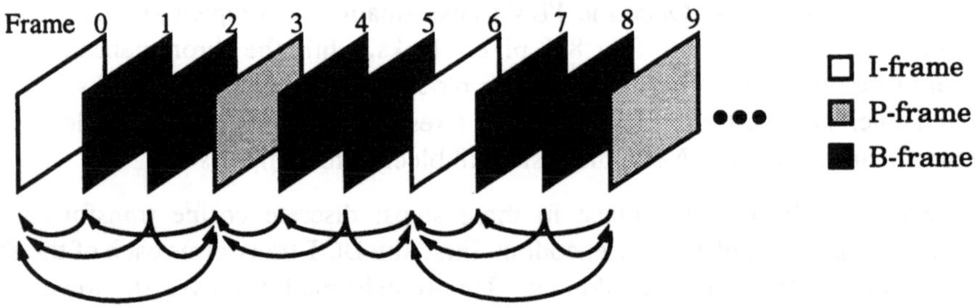

Figure 2.3: MPEG Frame Dependencies. This figure shows the frame dependencies for the macroblocks within an MPEG encoded video stream. The actual pattern of these frame types may vary depending on the amount of random access required.

compressed video stream that has a bit rate of approximately 1.5 Mbit/second. To support future broadcast quality video, the MPEG-2 video standard results in the compression of 720x480 video at 60 frames per second into a stream of 4 to 10 Mbits[ROWE94]. The standard itself specifies a syntax that all MPEG encoded streams must follow, but within the standard there are many different encoding schemes that can be used.

At a high level, MPEG video sequences consist of several different layers that provide the ability to randomly access a video sequence as well as provide a barrier against corrupted information. The six layers within MPEG are shown in Table 2.1 along with their main functions within the standard.

All MPEG frames are encoded in one of three different ways: Intra-encoded (I-Frames), Predictive-coded (P-Frames), or Bidirectionally-predictive-coded (B-Frames). As shown in Figure 2.3, each frame type in an MPEG stream can depend on up to two other frames, trading off degree of compression for random access and computation. I-frames are encoded as discrete frames, independent of adjacent

Frame Type	Types of macroblock encodings				
	intra	forward	backward	bidirectional	skipped
I	✓				
P	✓	✓			✓
B	✓	✓	✓	✓	✓

Table 2.2: MPEG Macroblock Encodings. This table shows the possible macroblock encodings for different frame types. I frames have no dependencies and each macroblock must be intra-coded. P frames can have up to 4 macroblock dependencies with non-zero motion vectors, while B frames can have up to 8 macroblock dependencies if bidirectionally encoded.

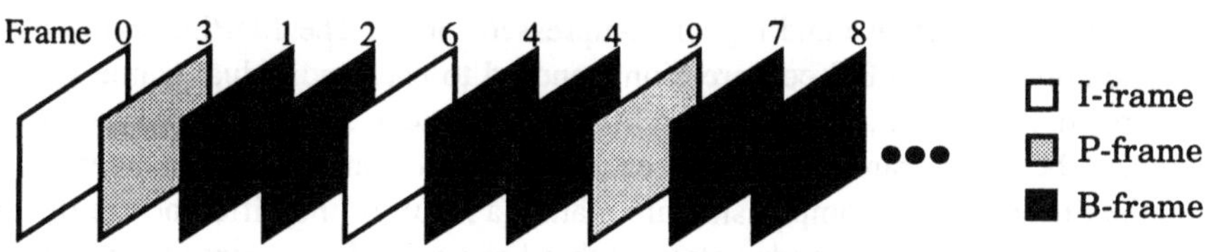

Figure 2.4: MPEG Encoding Order. This figure shows the actual ordering of the compressed frames within the MPEG encoded video stream for the sample clip shown in Figure 2.3.

frames. Thus they provide randomly accessible points within the video stream. Because of this, I-frames have the worst compression ratio of the three frame types. P-frames are coded with respect to a past I-frame or P-frame. The B-frames require a preceding and a following frame, which may be either I-frames or P-frames, in order to be decoded, but they offer the highest degree of compression. To allow for maximal compression and quality of picture, the individual macroblocks within B and P-frames may also be coded in several ways depending on the correlation of the macroblock to the frames on which they depend (seeTable 2.2). A macroblock in a B-frame, for example, can be encoded in one of five ways. All macroblocks can be intra-encoded (stand-alone) if there is not a high enough correlation with the frames on which they can be dependent on. Because the B-frames can depend on frames in the future, when encoding, the MPEG stream is rearranged so that the dependent frames are placed after the frames that they depend on. Figure 2.4 shows the reordering that occurs for the sample clip from Figure 2.3. For clarity of discussion, we refer to the frames upon which the P and B frames depend as *key* frames.

The Group of Pictures Layer (GOP) allows the user to group together any arbitrary number of frames starting with an I-frame. The GOP is a self-contained unit and therefore can be viewed by itself without looking at the GOPs surrounding it in the sequence. For MPEG encoded videos with multiple frame types, each GOP is generally set to start on every I frame. Thus, the example clip shown in Figure 2.3 is generally encoded with 6 frames per GOP. The actual number of frames required by each GOP, however, can vary and is not fixed by the MPEG standard.

Our research is mainly focused at the picture level for the delivery of compressed video across networks, and at the macroblock level for the reconstruction of MPEG video in software. To fully understand the lower layers of MPEG encoding, we refer readers to the MPEG compression standard which provides information down to bit level of how MPEG is encoded [CCIT93]. A higher level description of MPEG can be found in [LEGA91].

2.3 Video Compression and Burstiness

An understanding of how burstiness is introduced into a video stream can provide insight into the effective handling of compressed video. The MJPEG compression technique applies the JPEG compression standard to each individual frame within a video stream. As a result, the burstiness in a MJPEG video stream is purely a result of differences between frames. Because each macroblock must have an average DC value, the differences in compression are mainly a result of the difference in the high frequency components. For video streams that have roughly the same scene content, such as a typical video conference or lecture, the bit rate generated by MJPEG is fairly stable. As an example, consider the video sequence shown in Figure 2.5. The *Seminar* video consists of a speaker standing in front of an overhead projector presenting a talk. The inverted spikes that occur fairly regularly are a result of the speaker removing a transparency from the overhead projector, thus eliminating the need for a lot of high frequency components to represent the words and figures from the overhead projector. As a result, the difference in the various levels in the *Seminar* video are due to the transparencies and not the movement of the speaker. On the other hand, videos that have many different scenes generally have more burstiness due to the larger varying amounts of high frequency data. As an example, the movie *Speed* (see Figure 2.6) has frame averages that covered a wide range of bit-rates.

Because MPEG video compression techniques uses the same basic DCT compression algorithm as JPEG, the bit-rates for an all I-encoded video are similar to those of a MJPEG compressed video. To take advantage of temporal correlation between frames, MPEG compressed videos usually consist of a fixed pattern of I, P and B frames. While the use of P and B frames typically cause burstiness within the pattern, they do not really affect the long-term burstiness of the video data for two reasons. First, the P and B frames generally require fewer bits to represent, which results in a smaller variation within each frame type (P and B). Second, the frame sizes of P and B frames are not correlated with the sizes of their key I frame. This stems from the fact that good motion compensation techniques remove much of the high frequency

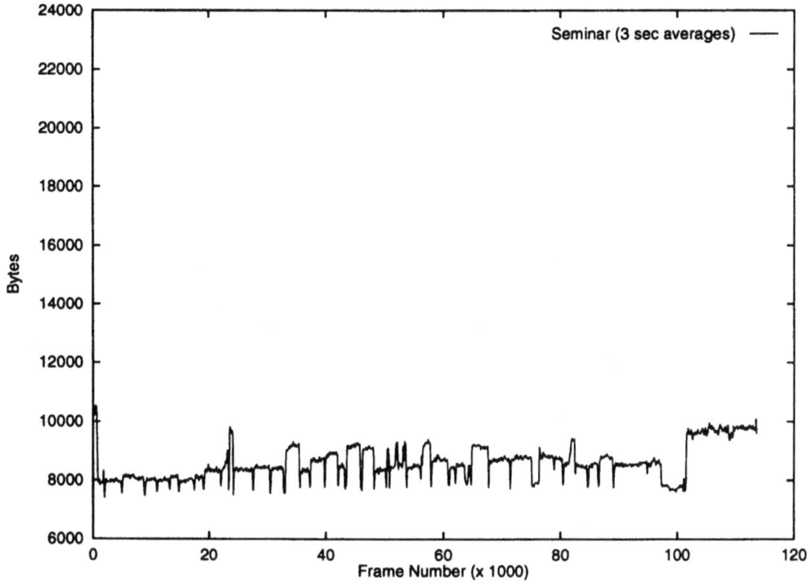

Figure 2.5: Seminar Example. This figure shows the 3 second frame averages (in Bytes) for a video recording of a MJPEG compressed (320x240 @ 30 fps, 90 quality) seminar. This seminar shows a speaker presenting the seminar on an overhead projector with transparencies.

data. As a result most of the bits in the frame are devoted to encoding vectors that represent the motion of the macroblocks between frames. Figure 2.7 shows how the pattern burstiness introduced by MPEG P and B frames differs from the long-term burstiness. In particular, note that the B-frames within the MPEG-encoded clip have a very small variance.

2.4 A Video Capture Testbed

In performing our experiments for this dissertation, we were interested in how the smoothing of bandwidth requirements for a single video affects the underlying services as well as how the interactions between videos may affect the utilization of the underlying network. In order to effectively test these, we required a video capture testbed capable of capturing a large amount of video data. In addition, capturing large amounts of video allowed us to study the differences that varying subjects of video had on compression and the burstiness that they introduced into the video stream. Using this PC-based test bed, we were able to capture many videos of varying length and subject material for our video library.

Our PC testbed consists of a Pioneer Laser Disc player, a MiroVideo DC1tv capture board, and a Pentium 90 processor with 32 MB of memory. The MiroVideo Capture

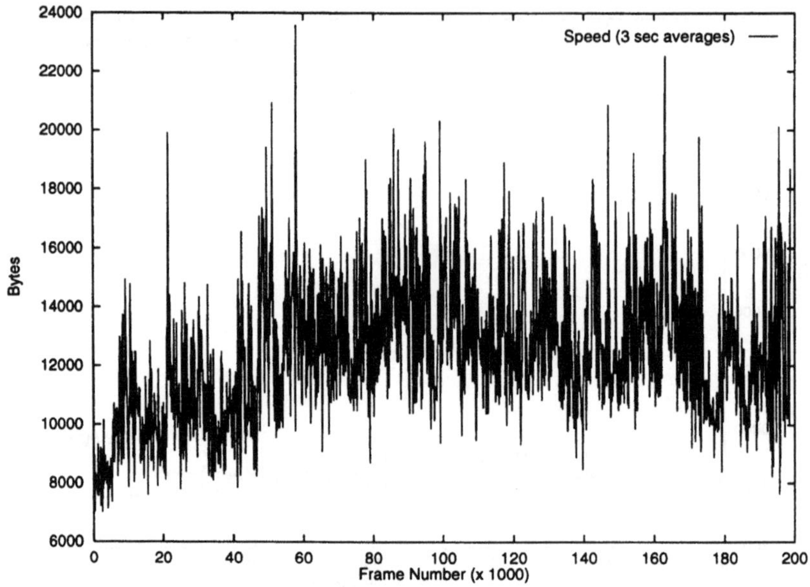

Figure 2.6: Movie Example. This figure shows the 3 second frame averages (in Bytes) for the movie *Speed* MJPEG compressed (320x240 @ 30 fps, 90 quality).

board is a Motion-JPEG compression board containing the C-Cube Microsystems' Motion-JPEG chip, the CL550. Because the smoothing algorithms we introduce are most sensitive to the changes in scene content, we felt the additional (order of magnitude) cost for a real-time MPEG encoder would not significantly change our results. Furthermore, because the basic routine for encoding I-frames within an MPEG video are based on the JPEG compression standard, the frame sizes for our experimental video data are roughly equivalent to all I-frame encoded MPEG video movies. The MiroVideo board digitized the movies at 640x480 and then subsampled them to 320x240 with guaranteed VHS picture quality.

2.5 A Video Library

Using our PC video capture testbed, we digitized 20 video clips, representing 31 hours of video, which totalled 38.5 GBytes of JPEG-compressed video data. In digitizing the video data, we attempted to capture a variety of different movies in order to have a fairly representative set of movies that might be handled. The *Beauty and the Beast* video is an animated Walt Disney movie, resulting in scenes with a lot of high frequency components as well as scenes that had large areas of constant color. The *1993 NCAA Final Four* video is a documentary describing the NCAA Final Four basketball tournament, resulting in many scenes with lots of detail. As a result, the *1993 NCAA Final Four* video had the highest average bit rate. In addition, we captured sev-

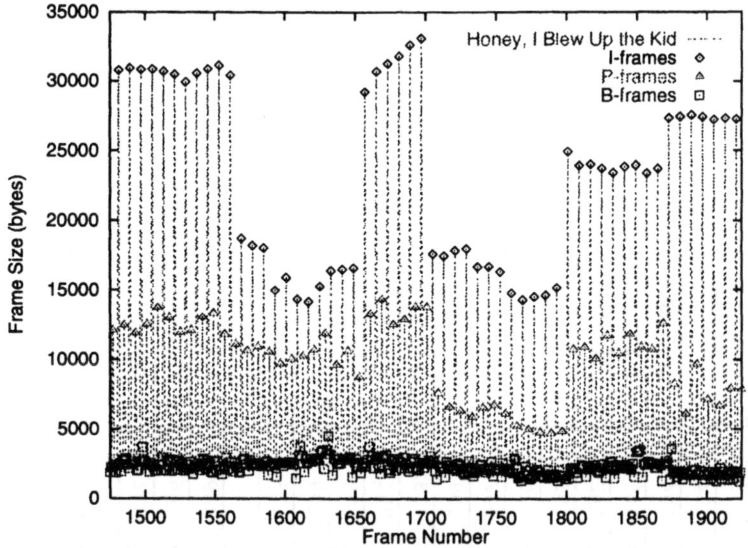

Figure 2.7: Burstiness Example. This figure shows how burstiness is introduced in a sample MPEG-encoded video clip from the Walt Disney movie *Honey, I Blew Up the Kid.* Pattern burstiness is introduced as a result of the encoding pattern (i.e. I, P, and B frames). Scene burstiness (or long term burstiness) is the burstiness between the different scenes within the movie. The scene burstiness is exhibited by the differences in the I-frames.

eral seminars and lectures to study the compression of "educational" videos. Because these videos were single scene videos, they resulted in the smallest variation in frame sizes. The rest of the movies are a mix of conventional entertainment containing a wide range of scene content, including digital effects and animations. As can be seen by the statistics for these movies found in Table 2.3, the captured data resulted in a wide range of compression ratios. Table 2.3 also shows that the bit-rates for these Motion-JPEG encoded movies were higher than the bit-rate specified for the MPEG video standard.

The 64 frequency components of the 8x8 block produced by the DCT algorithm are quantized at a level of coarseness determined by a quantization matrix. This matrix can be adjusted by scaling an overall picture quality factor. We captured the movie *E.T. - the Extra Terrestrial* at three different qualities, 75, 90, and 100. These numbers do not express linearly the quality that is seen by the user. For our sample *E.T.* video, picture qualities of 75, 90, and 100 resulted in bits per pixel measurements of 0.66, 0.94, and 1.64 bits per pixel, respectively. According to an introductory JPEG paper, 0.66 bits per pixel corresponds to "good to very good" quality, 0.94 bits per pixel corresponds to "excellent" picture quality, and 1.64 bits per pixel corresponds to a quality that is "usually indistinguishable from the original" [WALL91].

Title	Quality	Total Size (GBytes)	Length (min)	Ave. Size (bytes)	Largest Frame	Smallest Frame	Mbps	Std. Dev.
Beauty and Beast	90	1.82	80	12661	30367	2701	3.04	3580
Big	90	2.26	102	12346	23485	1503	2.96	2366
Crocodile Dundee	90	1.82	94	10773	19439	1263	2.59	2336
E.T.	100	3.11	110	15749	30553	6827	3.78	3294
E.T.	75	1.24	110	6305	14269	1511	1.51	1840
E.T.	90	1.78	110	9022	19961	2333	2.17	2574
Home Alone 2	90	2.35	115	11383	22009	3583	2.73	2480
Honey, I Blew Up the Kid	90	2.12	85	13836	23291	3789	3.32	3183
Hot Shots 2	90	1.92	84	12766	29933	3379	3.06	3240
Jurassic Park	90	2.50	122	11363	23883	1267	2.73	3252
Junior	90	2.71	107	14013	25119	1197	3.36	3188
Rookie of the Year	90	2.22	99	12435	27877	3531	2.98	2731
Seminar	90	0.98	63	8604	10977	7181	2.07	592
Seminar2	90	1.08	68	8835	12309	1103	2.12	608
Seminar3	90	0.88	52	9426	11167	7152	2.26	690
Sister Act	90	2.06	96	11902	24907	1457	2.86	2608
Sleepless in Seattle	90	1.72	101	9477	16617	3207	2.28	2459
Speed	90	2.46	110	12374	29485	2741	2.97	2707
Total Recall	90	2.34	109	11978	24769	2741	2.88	2692
1993 NCAA Final Four	90	1.21	41	16456	29565	2565	3.95	4138

Table 2.3: Video Movie Library Statistics. This table shows the statistics that were gathered for the video clips in our video movie library.

For comparison of the different movies, we have graphed the 3 second frame averages for all the movies digitized (Figure 2.8 to Figure 2.27). These graphs show the pattern of variation within each movie and how the burstiness was introduced. Note the low variation in the three seminar videos in contrast to the other videos.

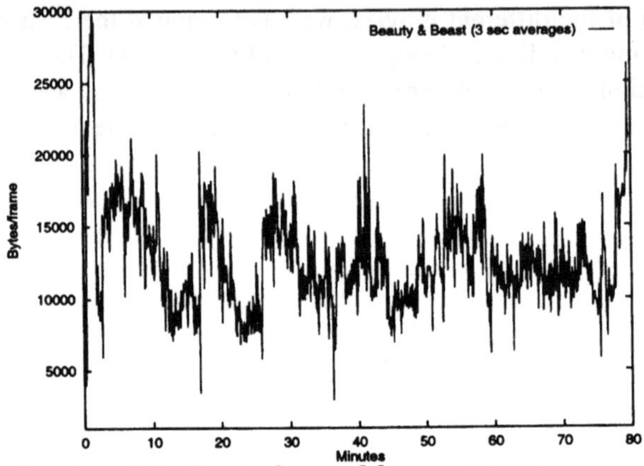

Figure 2.8: ***Beauty and the Beast*** **- 3 second frame averages.**

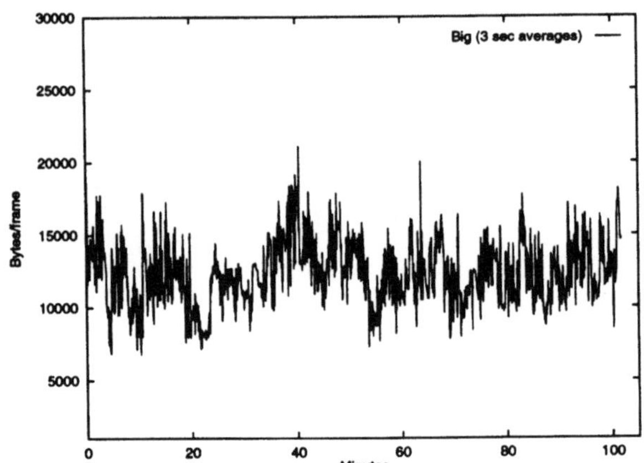

Figure 2.9: ***Big*** **- 3 second frame averages.**

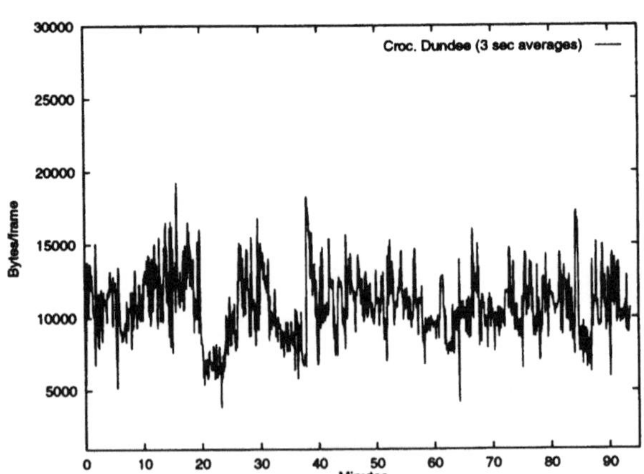

Figure 2.10: ***Crocodile Dundee*** **- 3 second frame averages.**

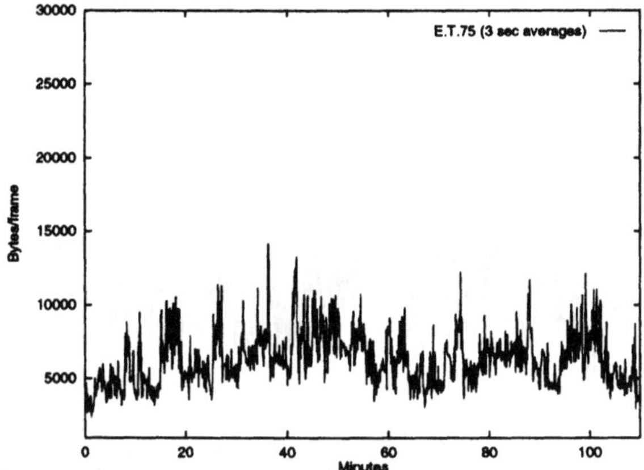

Figure 2.11: ***E.T.*** **(Quality 75) - 3 second frame averages.**

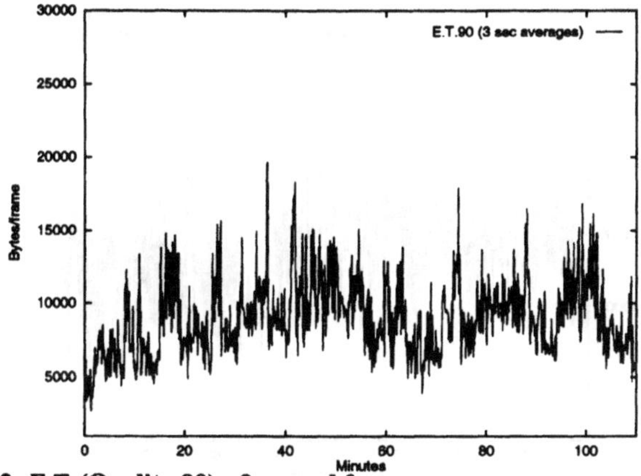

Figure 2.12: ***E.T.*** **(Quality 90) - 3 second frame averages.**

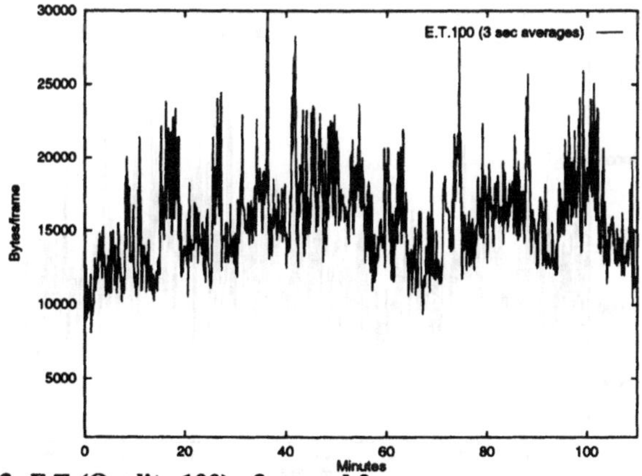

Figure 2.13: ***E.T.*** **(Quality 100) - 3 second frame averages.**

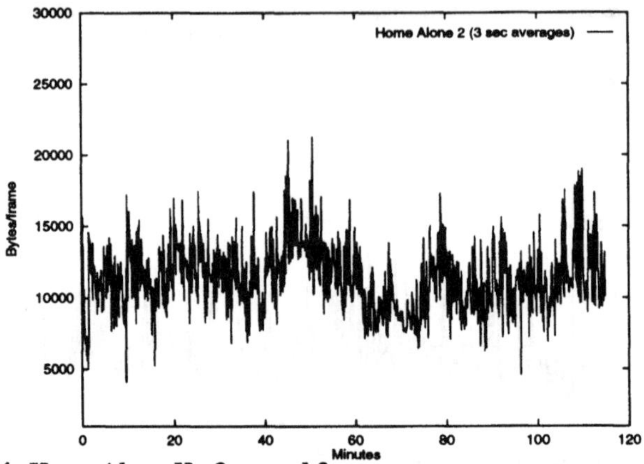

Figure 2.14: ***Home Alone II*** **- 3 second frame averages.**

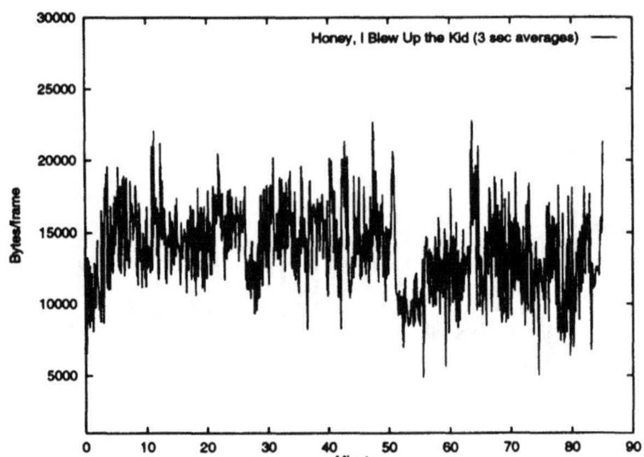

Figure 2.15: ***Honey, I Blew Up the Kid*** **- 3 second frame averages.**

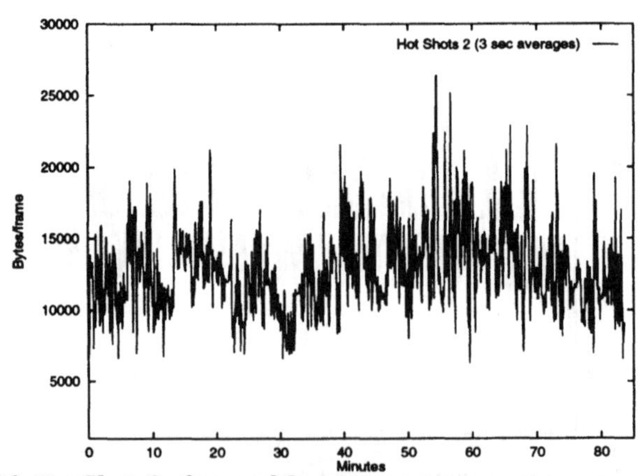

Figure 2.16: ***Hot Shots 2*** **- 3 second frame averages.**

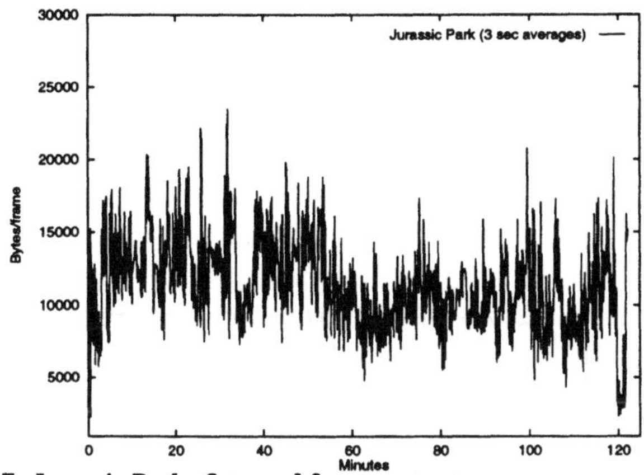

Figure 2.17: ***Jurassic Park*** **- 3 second frame averages.**

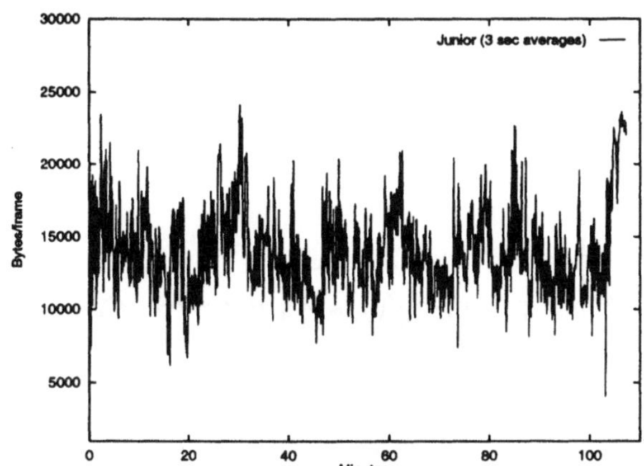

Figure 2.18: ***Junior*** **- 3 second frame averages.**

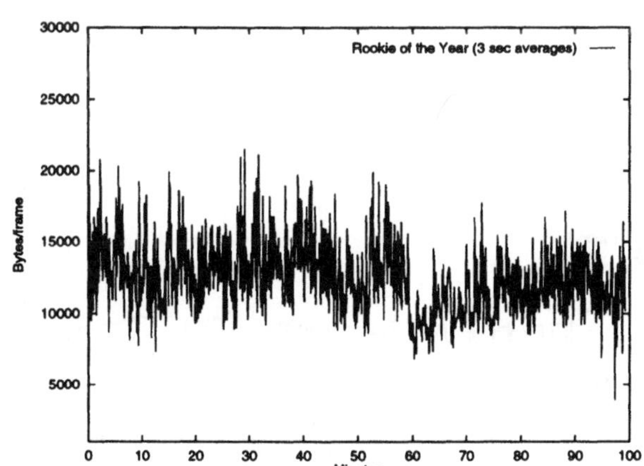

Figure 2.19: ***Rookie of the Year*** **- 3 second frame averages.**

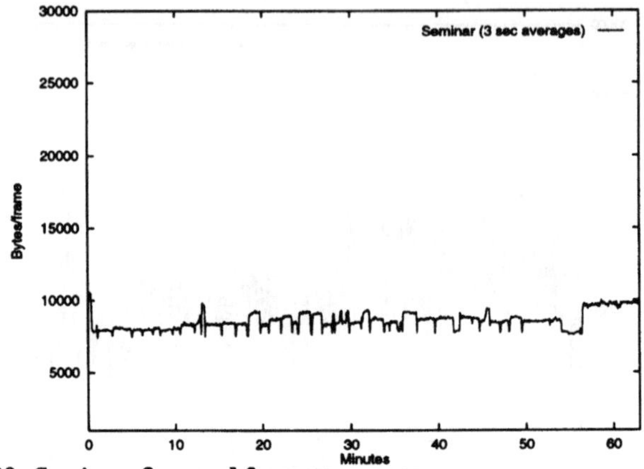

Figure 2.20: ***Seminar*** **-3 second frame averages.**

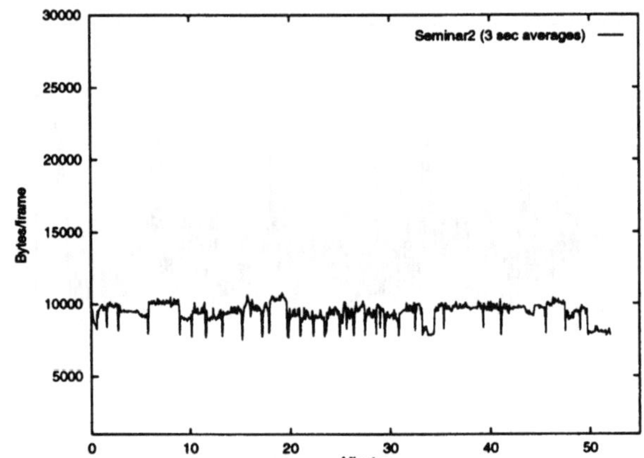

Figure 2.21: ***Seminar2*** **-3 second frame averages.**

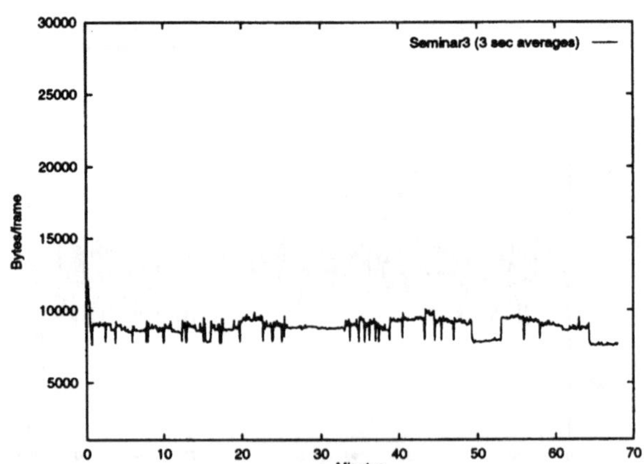

Figure 2.22: ***Seminar3*** **-3 second frame averages.**

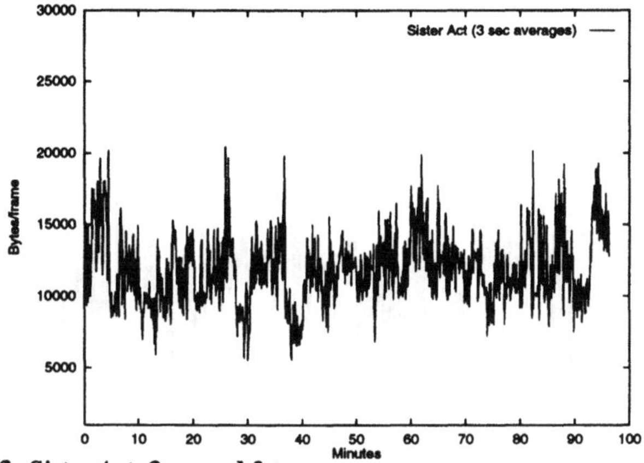

Figure 2.23: ***Sister Act*** **-3 second frame averages.**

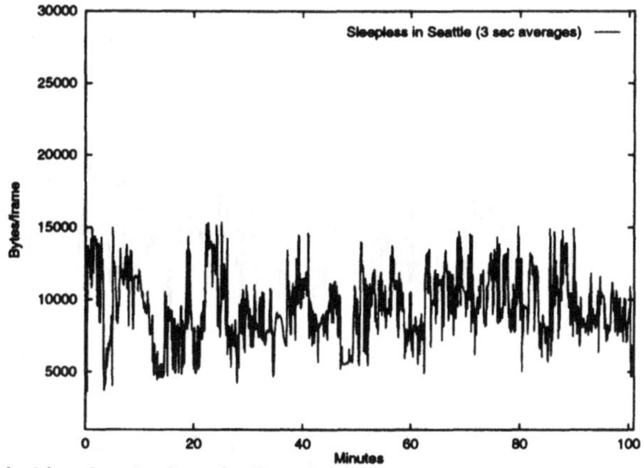

Figure 2.24: ***Sleepless in Seattle*** **-3 second frame averages.**

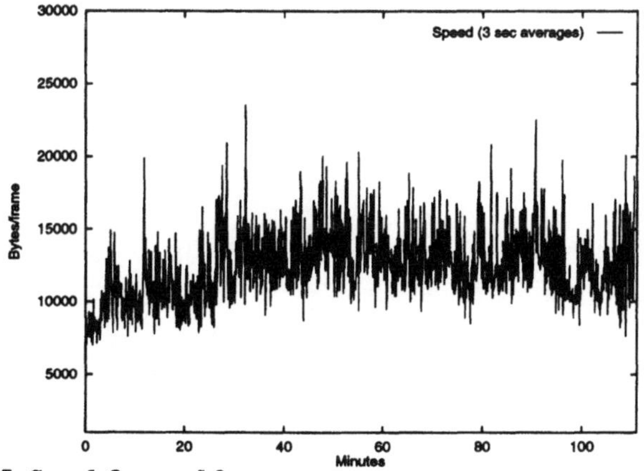

Figure 2.25: ***Speed*** **-3 second frame averages.**

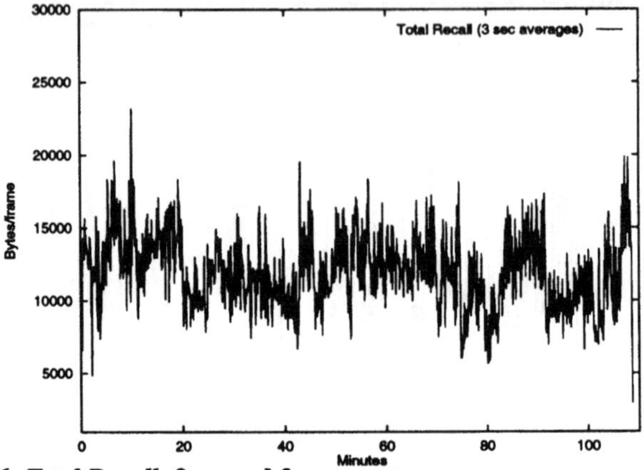

Figure 2.26: ***Total Recall*** **-3 second frame averages.**

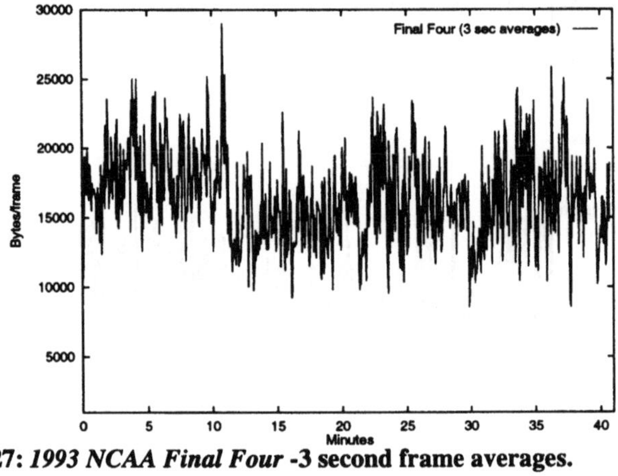

Figure 2.27: ***1993 NCAA Final Four*** **-3 second frame averages.**

3

BANDWIDTH SMOOTHING ALGORITHMS

3.1 Introduction

In this chapter, we address the issues involved with smoothing the bandwidth requirements for a single stream of video data. Video applications, such as video-on-demand services, rely on both high-speed networking and data compression. Data compression can introduce burstiness into video data streams, which complicates the problem of network resource management. For live-video applications, the problem of video delivery is constrained by the requirement that decisions must be made on-line and that the delay between sender and receiver must be limited. As a result, live-video applications may have to settle for weakened guarantees of service or for some degradation in quality of service. Work on problems raised by the requirements of live video includes work on statistical multiplexing [COHE94, REIN93], smoothing in exchange for delay [WALL91], jitter control [PARE92, JEFF92], and adjusting the quality of service to fit the resources available [PANC94, PANC92]. For stored video applications, the system can take a flexible approach to the latency of data delivery. In particular, it can make use of buffering to smooth the burstiness introduced by data compression. Because the entire video stream is known *a priori*, it is possible to calculate a complete plan for the delivery of the video data that avoids both the loss of picture quality and the wasting of network bandwidth through overstatement of bandwidth requirements.

The utility of prefetching is quite simple to explain. Since the bytes for any given frame can be supplied either by the network or by a prefetch buffer, the burstiness of the network bandwidth requirement can be compensated for by filling the prefetch buffer in advance of each burst, by delivering more bytes than needed across the network, and draining it in the course of the burst. The size of the prefetch buffer determines the size of burst that can be averaged out in this way. With a small buffer, only a limited amount of data can be prefetched without overflowing the buffer, so the bandwidth required of the network may remain relatively bursty. With a larger buffer, there is the possibility that most of the burstiness of a video clip can be eliminated through prefetching. This, however, requires a plan for prefetching the data that ensures that the large buffer is filled in advance of bursts that place a high demand upon the buffer.

In this chapter, we examine how the addition of a smoothing buffer can smooth the necessary bandwidth requirements from the underlying network for a single video stream. We present smoothing techniques that fall into two broad categories: window-based and non-window-based smoothing techniques. We refer to algorithms that smooth bandwidth based on some maximum number of frames as *window based* smoothing algorithms. On the other hand, we refer to algorithms which make smoothing decisions based on the size of the smoothing buffer alone as *non-window* based smoothing techniques. We introduce the notion of *critical bandwidth allocation* for the delivery of compressed prerecorded video. This algorithm minimizes the number of bandwidth increases as well as the peak bandwidth requirement for the continuous playback of stored video. In addition to the critical bandwidth algorithm, we present an *optimal bandwidth allocation* algorithm that also minimizes the total number of changes required to play back stored video.

We present the window-based and non-window-based smoothing techniques in Section 3.2 and Section 3.4, respectively. In these sections we state the theorems that apply to the use of the critical bandwidth techniques. In Section 3.4, we compare the various smoothing algorithms and demonstrate the key differences between the algorithms. Finally, we summarize our findings in Section 3.5

3.2 Window-Based Smoothing Algorithms

In this section, we describe two window-based smoothing algorithms for the delivery of video data. Because these algorithms smooth bandwidth based on a set number of frames (or window size), the maximum amount of prefetch is determined by both the window size and the size of the buffer used for smoothing. The window size can be picked to be a multiple of the video encoding pattern for MPEG compressed video or can be a multiple of the bandwidth allocation unit of the underlying link layer. Window-based smoothing is particularly suitable for use in live video conferencing applications because they result in a maximum delay proportional to the window size.

3.2.1 Average Bandwidth Allocation

A simple window-based method for easing bandwidth fluctuations is to group some number of frames together into a *chunk* and send the frames across the network at the average bandwidth requirement for the chunk. The use of averaging algorithms has been proposed for both live and stored video applications [LAM94,VIN94]. By using this method, clients can guarantee that the bandwidth needed is constant throughout

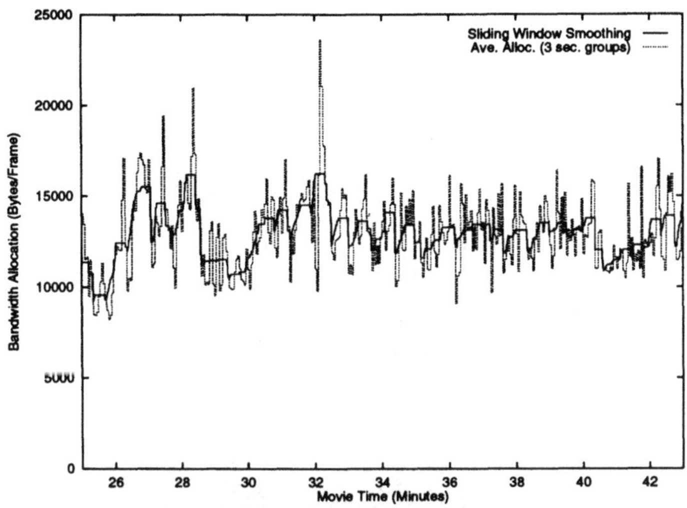

Figure 3.1: Average Bandwidth Allocation vs. Sliding Window Smoothing. Each line in the graph represents a sample of bandwidth requests from an 18 minute sample from the movie *Speed*. Each algorithm was run assuming a maximum buffer size of 2 MBytes. The sliding window smoothing algorithm was applied to 45 frame chunks and a window size of 11 chunks.

the chunk. The amount of smoothing, however, is directly related to the chunk size. Using this constant bandwidth for the entire chunk implies that the end user is not guaranteed that local buffer starvation does not occur during the display of the chunk unless it has buffered at least one chunk ahead. The end user is, however, guaranteed that the maximum delay between the transmission and playback of the video is proportional to the chunk size used. For stored video applications, this maximum delay is twice the size of the chunk. Using bandwidth smoothing with very large chunk sizes becomes impractical because of this buffering requirement. In addition, because this algorithm merely groups a fixed number of frames together, no smoothing occurs across chunks. A sample bandwidth allocation graph using the average allocation algorithm is shown in Figure 3.1.

3.2.2 Sliding Window Smoothing

Rather than simply averaging within fixed chunks, a sliding window can be used to smooth within a larger region. A moving window of *n* chunks is smoothed by shifting large bandwidth requirements in a chunk to earlier chunks (within the window) that stand below the average for the window as a whole. Thus, for a window of size *n* chunks, the bandwidth allocation for a chunk *i* is set to the average of all the frames in chunk *i* to chunk *i+n-1*. For chunk *i+1*, the bandwidth allocation is set to the average of all the frames in chunk *i+1* to chunk *i+n*. This averaging has the effect of causing the data to be prefetched in advance of bursts of large frames. However, redistribution is limited by the size of the window, so peaks and valleys will still occur.

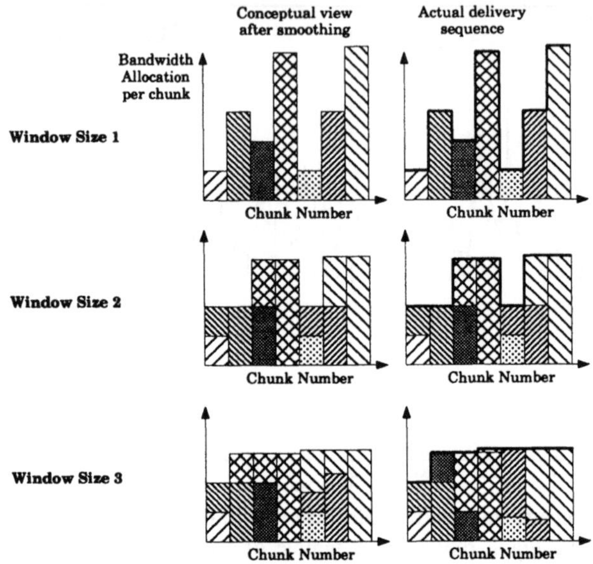

Figure 3.2: Sliding Window Smoothing Example. This figure shows the affect that the window size has on the smoothing for the sliding window smoothing algorithm. The heavy solid lines on the right represent the bandwidth allocation plans that are made. Note how the window size (particularly for the window size of 1 and 2) limits the amount of smoothing to the window.

Figure 3.2 shows the affect that changing the window size has for the sliding window smoothing algorithm.The amount of smoothing is determined by the window size. A window size of 1 yields no smoothing at all and the graphs are equivalent to the average bandwidth allocation algorithm. With sufficiently large windows considerable smoothing is possible. This smoothing is accomplished through prefetching and requires buffer space in the receiver, but far less than would be required to achieve equivalent smoothing with the average allocation algorithm. Figure 3.1 shows a sample sliding window bandwidth allocation plan for the movie *Speed* compared with the average allocation algorithm.

Sliding window smoothing, however, has some drawbacks for planning bandwidth allocation. While the number of adjustments in bandwidth is less than required for the average allocation algorithm, frequent adjustments are still necessary. Furthermore, rises in bandwidth are generally accomplished in several steps, each possibly requiring negotiation with the network manager.

3.3 Non-Window-Based Smoothing Algorithms

While window-based smoothing algorithms are suitable for live-video applications because they have a maximum delay between transmission and playback, they may not take full advantage of the buffer available for smoothing. Because the constraints between transmission and playback are relaxed for stored-video, creating *a priori* bandwidth plans that maximize the usage of the buffer allows the network management to be made simpler. In this section, we introduce the notion of *critical bandwidth allocation* for stored video playback. These algorithms base the bandwidth allocation decisions based on the *a priori* knowledge of the video frames that are available. By taking advantage of this knowledge, a bandwidth plan for retrieval that minimizes the range of bandwidth values for playback is possible.

3.3.1 Taking Advantage of *A Priori* Information

Given a stored video stream consisting of n frames, where each frame i requires f_i bytes of storage, we can create a *bandwidth plan* for the delivery of the video from the server to the client *before* the transmission of data begins. In order to provide continuous playback on the client side, the server must always transmit quickly enough to avoid buffer underflow, where

$$F_{under}(k) = \sum_{i=0}^{k} f_i$$

indicates the amount of data consumed at the client by frame k, where $k=0,1,\ldots n-1$. In order to provide continuous playback, we note that the client must receive greater than $F_{under}(k)$ bytes of data by frame k. That is,

$$F_{under}(k) \le \sum_{i=0}^{k} c_i$$

where c_i is the transmission rate during frame i of the smoothed video stream. Figure 3.3 shows two possible bandwidth plans for the continuous delivery of data from the server to the client, one where bandwidth is plentiful and the other where bandwidth may be limited. The maximum vertical distance from the bandwidth plan to $F_{under}()$ determines the minimum buffer required to use the bandwidth plan.

In situations where the client may have some limited buffer resources, the bandwidth plan should be created such that the client does not receive more data than

$$F_{over}(k) = \sum_{i=0}^{k} f_i + b$$

by frame k, to prevent overflow of the playback buffer (of size b). Consequently, any valid server transmission plan should stay within the river outlined by these vertically equidistant functions. That is,

$$F_{under}(k) \le \sum_{i=0}^{k} c_i \le F_{over}(k)$$

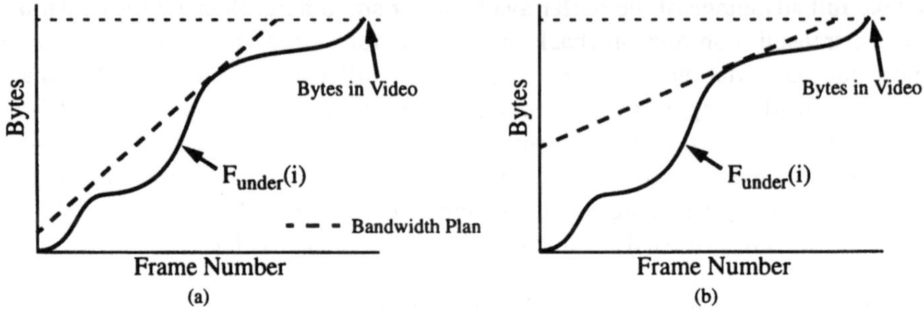

Figure 3.3: Bandwidth Plan Example. Figure (a) shows a bandwidth plan for the continuous delivery of video using a *single* constant bandwidth allocation, minimizing the *maximum* vertical distance that the bandwidth plan deviates from $F_{under}()$. Figure (b) shows an example where the bandwidth resources may be limited. The y-intercept of the bandwidth plan determines how much data (and hence delay) the client must prefetch before playback can begin.

where c_i is the transmission rate during frame slot i of the smoothed video stream. We examine techniques for creating bandwidth plans under limited buffer sizes in Section 3.3.3 and Section 3.3.4.

3.3.2 Critical Bandwidth Allocation

The critical bandwidth allocation algorithm without regard to the smoothing buffer size creates a bandwidth allocation plan for video data which contains *no increases* in bandwidth requirements for continuous playback and does not require any prefetching of data before playback can begin. By calculating such a bandwidth plan, admission control is greatly simplified. That is, the network manager needs to only ask - "*Is there enough bandwidth to start the flow of data?*". Because the CBA algorithm only calculates the minimum bandwidths that are necessary for continuous playback, the buffer size requirement for continuous playback, may be fairly substantial. The buffer size requirement, however, is generally not as large as one required by a single constant bandwidth allocation for the entire video. Finally, the CBA algorithms result in a bandwidth plan that (1) does not require prefetching (and, hence, delay) for playback to begin, and (2) results in a monotonically decreasing sequence of bandwidth allocations. For clarity, we say that a bandwidth allocation plan consists of *runs* of constant bandwidth allocations.

We can describe the intuition behind the CBA algorithm with our geometric model from the last section. Given the function $F_{under}()$ for a video, the critical bandwidth allocation algorithm allocates a decreasing sequence of constant bandwidths at the minimum bandwidths necessary to play back the video without buffer underflow. This corresponds to creating a convex arc from the beginning of the movie to the end of the movie with each run starting and ending on the function F_{under}(i), where the slope

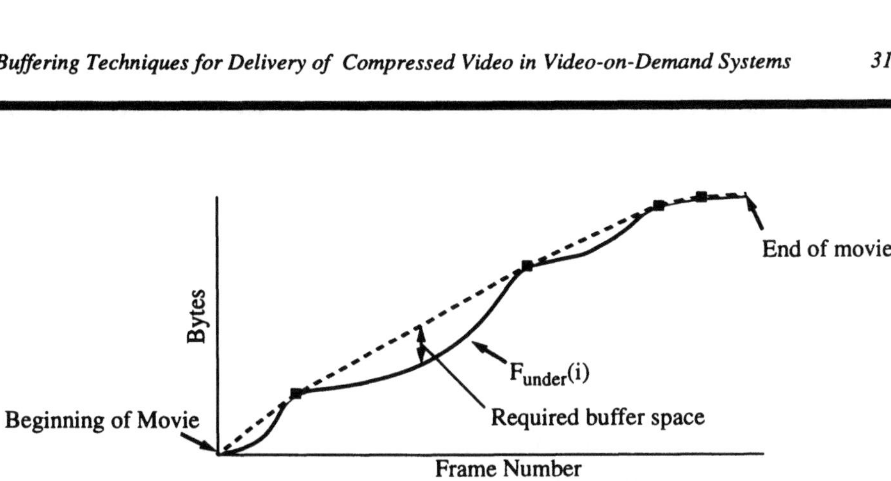

Figure 3.4: Critical Bandwidth Allocation Example. The solid line in the graph shows a possible graph for $F_{under}(i)$, while the dotted line shows a plan determined by the CBA algorithm. This plan requires 5 decreases in bandwidth, where the squares on the dotted lines show the junctures between runs. The slope of each dotted line is the bandwidth requirement for that run. The minimum buffer size is represented by the maximum vertical distance between the critical bandwidth allocation plan and the function $F_{under}(i)$.

of each line (run) determines the bandwidth allocation that is required for that run. This is shown in Figure 3.4 as a convex arc around $F_{under}(i)$. While the CBA algorithm does not observe any limits in available buffer space, it does calculate the minimum necessary buffer to play the video clip with a single monotonically decreasing sequence of bandwidth allocations. The required buffer size is determined by the maximum vertical distance between the bandwidth allocation plan and the function $F_{under}(i)$. The magnitude of this minimum buffer size may vary for the same clip, depending on the encoding scheme used and the long term burstiness that results. Note that any constant bandwidth allocation plan for the entire movie must have this minimum buffer size but is typically much larger in size. This leads to the following theorem for the critical bandwidth allocation algorithm:

Theorem 1 : The critical bandwidth allocation algorithm with no buffer limitation results in a strictly decreasing sequence of bandwidth allocations

Proof: To prove this theorem, we start by proving that the critical bandwidth following the first critical point CP_0 must have a bandwidth CB less than the first critical bandwidth CB_0. To see that the run following CP_0 must have a critical bandwidth less than CP_0, assume that this run has a critical bandwidth CB determined by a critical point CP. By the definition of critical bandwidth, CB_0 must be greater than the average frame size from frame 1 to frame CP. This requires the following inequality to be true

$$CB_0 > \frac{(CP_0 \cdot CB_0) + (CP - CP_0)\,CB}{CP}$$

That is, CB_0 must be greater than the average of all frames from 0 to CP by definition. We then rewrite CP_0 as $[CP - (CP - CP_0)]$ and substitute it in the first term, leaving

$$CB_0 > \frac{(CP \cdot CB_0 - (CP - CP_0)\, CB_0) + (CP - CP_0)\, CB}{CP}$$

Then by rearrangement, this requires

$$CB_0 > CB_0 + \frac{(CP - CP_0)\,(CB - CB_0)}{CP}$$

to hold. Since CP is greater than CP_0, CB must be less than CB_0.
By recursively re-applying this to the remaining portion after CP_0, we see that the critical bandwidth algorithm must result in a monotonically decreasing sequence of bandwidth requirements.//

CBA Implementation

To algebraically create a CBA plan, let CB_0, CB_1, ..., CB_k be the runs created by the CBA algorithms, then the critical bandwidth CB_0, in bytes per frame, is defined as

$$CB_0 = \max_{1 \le i \le N} \left(\frac{\sum_{j=1}^{i} f_j}{j} \right)$$

where N is the number of frames in the video clip and $frame_j$ is the size in bytes of frame number j. Thus, the critical bandwidth is determined by the frame, i, for which the average frame size for i and all prior frames in the video clip is maximized. We call frame i, which sets the critical bandwidth, the *critical point* in the video clip, or CP_0. In the case where the maximum is achieved multiple times, we choose CP_0 to be the last frame at which it is achieved.

Starting at frame CP_0+1, we apply the definition of the *critical bandwidth* to the rest of the clip, resulting in CB_1 and CP_1. The critical bandwidths, CB_n, are determined by a sequence of critical point CP_n, where

$$CB_n = \max_{CP_{n-1} < i \le N} \left(\frac{\sum_{CP_{n-1}+1}^{i} f_j}{j} \right)$$

The use of the critical bandwidth allocation algorithm is an effective technique to use for systems that have appropriate amounts of buffering for several reasons. First, the playback of the video can commence immediately. Second, the admission control algorithm is simple - *Is there enough bandwidth to start the channel?* Third, these bandwidths are the minimum constant bandwidth necessary for continuous playback without requiring an increase in the bandwidth allocation. Finally, we note that is pos-

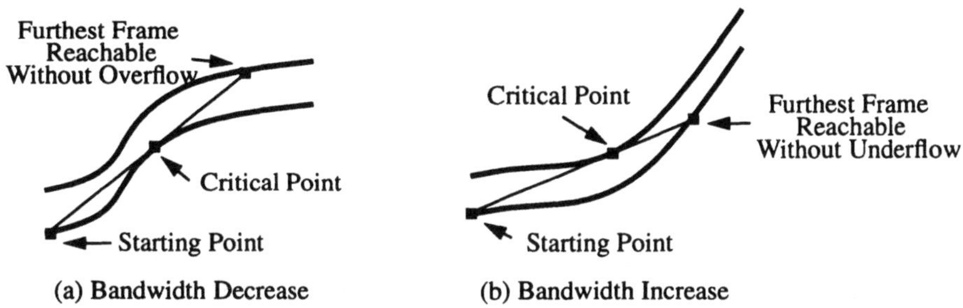

Figure 3.5: Critical Bandwidth and Critical Point Example. On the left is an example calculation of a critical point in which a bandwidth decrease is required in the next run, while on the right is a similar calculation for the case where a bandwidth increase is required in the following run.

sible to reduce the beginning bandwidth requirement by prefetching data for the initial run.

3.3.3 Critical Bandwidth Allocation with Maximum Buffer Constraint

Using the critical bandwidth algorithm results in the calculation of the minimum buffer size necessary to treat the entire video clip as a monotonically decreasing sequence of bandwidth allocations. In the event that this minimum buffer size exceeds the buffer space available, then the client must increase the bandwidth in the middle of the video clip, substituting increased network bandwidth for missing buffer bandwidth. The critical bandwidth allocation with a maximum buffer constraint has the same properties as the CBA algorithm but increases bandwidth *only when necessary*. As a result, the CBA algorithm with a maximum buffer constraint (referred to from now on as the CBA algorithm) results in a plan that:

- requires no prefetching of data before playback begins
- has the minimum number of bandwidth increase changes
- has the smallest peak bandwidth requirement
- has the largest minimum bandwidth requirement

In our discussion, we modify the definition of critical points and critical bandwidths to work with a maximum buffer constraint. Given some starting point and the buffer occupancy at the starting point, the critical bandwidth is the bandwidth such that the buffer limitations are not violated for the largest number of frames. Figure 3.5 shows two representative examples of critical points for runs that require a decrease and increase in bandwidth in the following run. As a result, for a run which requires a bandwidth increase in the *next* run, the critical point is determined by a point on $F_{over}(i)$, while for a run which requires a bandwidth decrease in the *next* run, the critical point is determined by a point on $F_{under}(i)$. Finally, as shown in Figure 3.5, we use the terms *hub* to refer to the part of the run that precedes the critical point and *frontier* to refer to the trajectory of the run past the critical point.

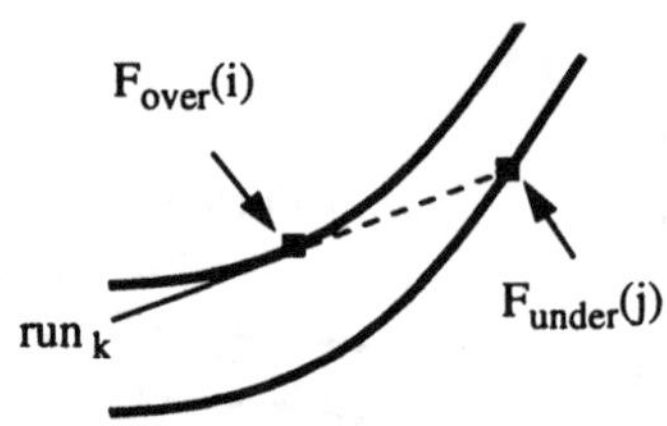

Figure 3.6: Bandwidth Increase Search Example. For the calculation of run k+1 a search is performed on the line connecting F_{over}(i) and F_{under}(j) to find a starting point such that the critical point for the next run is as far out in time as possible.

To create a bandwidth plan, the CBA algorithm starts at frame 0 with no initial buffer and calculates the critical bandwidth and critical point for the next run. Note we can generally reduce the initially high bandwidth requirement by starting with an initial buffer size > 0, but it requires that the start playback of video to be delayed. If the critical point is on F_{under}(i), then a decrease in bandwidth is required in the next run and the critical point is used as the starting point for the next run. If the critical point for the run is on F_{over}(i), then an increase in bandwidth is required in the next run (see Figure 3.5). For these increases, a search on the frontier of the run is performed for a starting point such that the next run results in a critical point that is as far out as possible (as shown in Figure 3.6). This search requires the calculation of an initial buffer occupancy between the maximum buffer size and 0 because the frontier of the run connects F_{over}(i) and F_{under}(i).

For a run *k+1* that requires an increase in bandwidth from the last run *k*, the bandwidth is allocated at a slope such that the run extends as far out in time as possible. To implement this, a search is performed at the end of run *k* along the frontier of run *k* as shown in Figure 3.6. The actual search algorithm is not of great importance in the usual case since these searches are relatively infrequent. One can choose to implement either a linear or binary search. This search results in one of two cases (if it is not the last run in the movie), either an increase or decrease in the bandwidth allocation is required for the next run. Examples of these are shown in Figure 3.7 and Figure 3.8, respectively. This results in the following two properties concerning the bandwidth increase search for a run *k*.

Property 1 : For a run k which (1) increases the bandwidth requirement over run k-1 and (2) requires an increase in bandwidth in run k+1, the search for run k results in a run which is determined by the slope between the points $F_{under}(m)$ and $F_{over}(n)$ where m < n.

This property essentially says that the search for run *k* as shown in Figure 3.7, which results in a bandwidth increase in run *k+1*, is defined by two points, one from F_{under}(i) and the other from F_{over}(i). In addition, because run *k+1* requires an increase in bandwidth, the frontier of run *k* must end on a point on F_{under}(i).

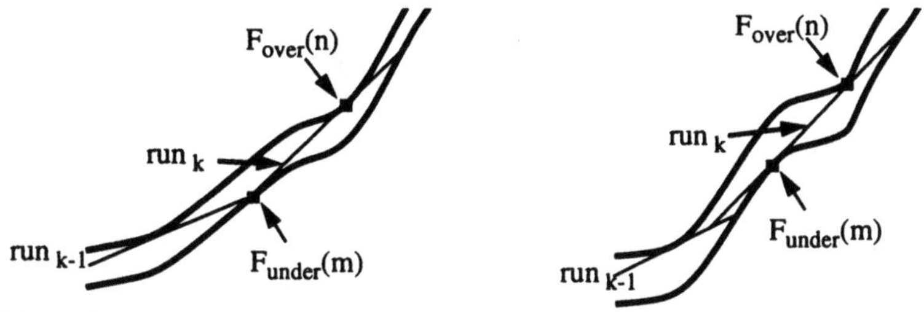

Figure 3.7: Bandwidth Search Example. This figure shows the two representative cases that arise when the search for run *k* results in another bandwidth increase required in run *k+1*. In (a), F_{under}(m) lies on the line created by run_{k-1}. In (b), F_{under}(m) does not lie on run *k-1*.

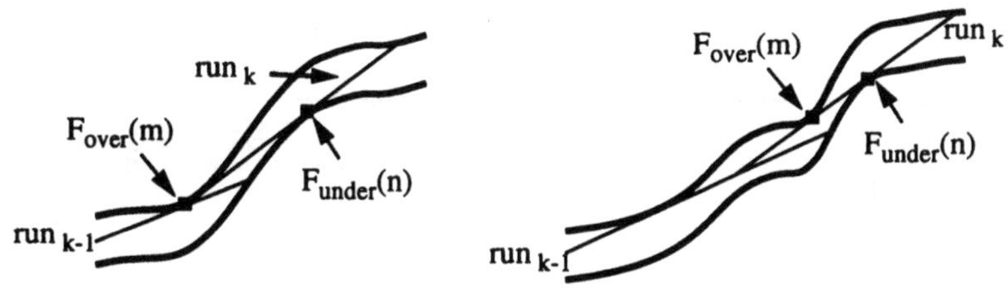

Figure 3.8: Bandwidth Search Example. This figure shows the two representative cases that arise when the search for run *k* will result in a bandwidth decrease required in run *k+1*. In (a), F_{under}(m) lies on the line created by run_{k-1}. In (b), F_{under}(m) does not lie on run *k-1*.

Property 2 : For a run k which (1) increases the bandwidth requirement over run k-1 and (2) requires an decrease in bandwidth in run k+1, the search for run k results in a run which is determined by a slope between the points $F_{over}(m)$ *and* $F_{under}(n)$*, where* $m < n$.

This property is the similar result for bandwidth decreases. That is, the search in run *k* is defined by two points, one from F_{over}(i) and the other from F_{under}(i). Figure 3.9 shows a sample construction using the critical bandwidth algorithm with maximum buffer constraint.

To recap, the CBA algorithm consists of allocating runs at their critical bandwidths. For bandwidth decreases, the end of the run is set to the critical point and the next run is started on the next frame. For bandwidth increases, a search is performed on the frontier of the last run to find a starting point such that the critical point of the next run is maximized. An example of critical bandwidth allocation smoothing can be found in Figure 3.10. Finally, by searching for a starting point such that the critical point is as far out in time as possible for bandwidth increases, an important theorem about the critical bandwidth algorithm can be derived:

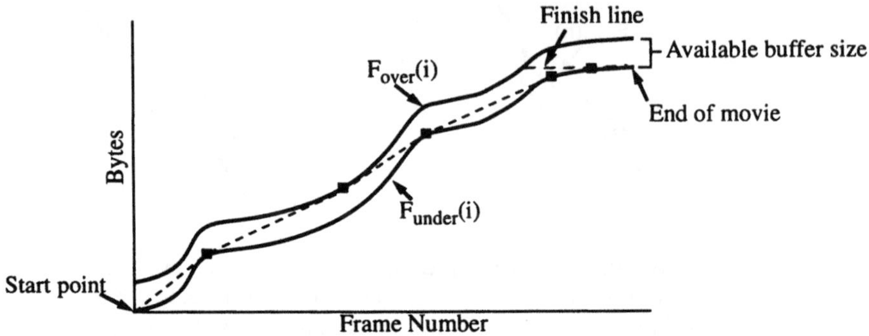

Figure 3.9: Critical Bandwidth Allocation with Maximum Buffer Example. This figure shows a sample construction of the CBA algorithm with a maximum buffer constraint. The dotted lines represent the runs within the bandwidth plan.

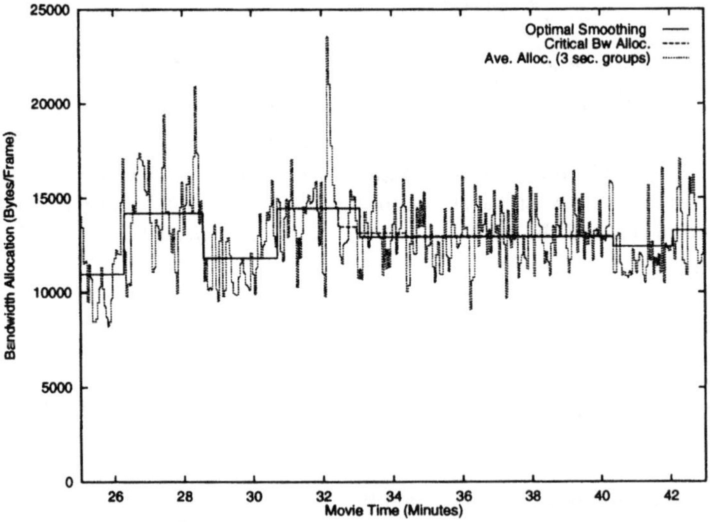

Figure 3.10: Critical Bandwidth Allocation vs. Optimal Bandwidth Allocation. This figure shows the same sample clip from the movie *Speed* as in Figure 3.1. The solid line shows the bandwidth allocation plan using the OBA algorithm and a 2 MB buffer, while the heavier dotted line shows the CBA algorithm. The main difference between the algorithms is that the OBA algorithm combines all the bandwidth decreases into a few request.

Theorem 2 : The critical bandwidth allocation algorithm with a fixed maximum buffer constraint results in a plan for playback of video without buffer starvation or buffer overflow with (1) the smallest number of bandwidth increases possible, (2) the minimum peak bandwidth requirement, and (3) the largest minimum bandwidth required.

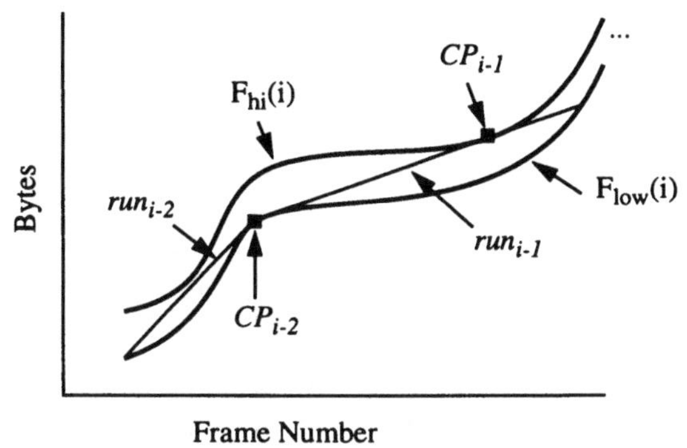

Figure 3.11: Bandwidth Decrease-Increase Example. This figure shows a run in a bandwidth allocation plan that decreases the bandwidth from the previous run and requires a bandwidth increase on the next run.

Proof: Let the CBA plan consist of *n* runs, each with a constant bandwidth allocation. We prove the above theorem by showing that all other plans must have (1) at least as many bandwidth increases, (2) cannot have a smaller peak bandwidth, and (3) cannot have a larger minimum bandwidth.

We first break the *n* runs into sets of consecutive runs which increase the bandwidth requirements from previous runs in the CBA plan. Let run *i* be the first run in each set, and let each set be numbered from *i* to *k*, $i<k$. Because run_i is the first run in a set of bandwidth increases, run *i-1* must have decreased the bandwidth over run *i-2*. This implies that run *i-2* was determined by a critical point on $F_{low}(i)$ and that run *i-1* starts on $F_{low}(i)$. In addition, the critical point for run *i-1* must be on $F_{hi}(i)$. This situation is shown in the figure below:.

We now note that because run *i-1* connect $F_{low}(i)$ and $F_{hi}(i)$, *any other* bandwidth plan not co-linear with run *i-1* must have a run that has a slope less than that chosen by run *i-1*. By showing this for all the sets of consecutive bandwidth increases, part 3 of the proof is shown. That is, any other bandwidth plan cannot have a higher minimum bandwidth than the CBA plan.

To show part 1 of the theorem (CBA results in the minimum number of bandwidth increases), we first consider run *i-1*. We note that any other plan not co-linear with run *i-1* must have a run that crosses run *i-1* with a lower bandwidth requirement (smaller slope) because run *i-1* connects $F_{low}(i)$ and $F_{hi}(i)$. As a result, any other plan *CANNOT* have a run that starts on or behind the hub of run *i-1* and cross the frontier for run *i-1*. Thus, any other bandwidth plan must also increase the bandwidth requirement before crossing the frontier of run *i-1* (see Figure 3.11). In the search for a run *i*, the CBA plan maximizes the distance reachable by run *i* by performing a search along the frontier of run *i-1*. Because any other bandwidth plan must increase its bandwidth *before* crossing the frontier of run *i-1*, it *CANNOT* cross the frontier created by run *i*, otherwise, the CBA algorithm would have found the same run in its search along the frontier of run *i-1*. Because at each step the other bandwidth plans also require an increase in bandwidth and can never pass the frontier created by that of the CBA plan, the set of consecutive increases is minimum. Applying this to all the sets of consecutive increases allows us to prove part 1 of the theorem. That is, the CBA plan results in the minimum number of bandwidth increases.

Finally, to show that the CBA results in the minimum peak bandwidth requirement, let us examine run *k* of each set of consecutive bandwidth increases. Because the set of runs are grouped into runs that consecutively increase the bandwidth requirements, run *k+1* must decrease the bandwidth requirement from run *k*. Using Property 2, we note that in the search for run *k* is performed along the frontier of run *k-1*, and that run *k* connects $F_{hi}(m)$ and $F_{low}(n)$ for some $m < n$. Because this run connect $F_{hi}(i)$ and $F_{low}(i)$, *any other* bandwidth plan no co-linear with run *k* must have a higher slope which crosses run *k*. By showing for each set of consecutive runs that other plans cannot have a minimum peak bandwidth less than the CBA plan, the CBA plan results in the minimum peak bandwidth requirement, thus, proving part 2 of the theorem. //

CBA Implementation

To algebraically calculate the CBA plan requires the allocation of individual runs. The calculation of a run requires the starting point for the run, $Frame_{start}$, and the initial buffer occupancy, $Buff_{init}$, at that starting point. To calculate a run starting from $Frame_{start}$ with initial buffer $Buff_{init}$, let

- $FrameAve_i$ be the average frame size from the beginning of the run to the *i*th frame within the run. This can be defined as:

$$FrameAve_i = \left(\frac{\left(\sum_{j = Frame_{start}}^{Frame_{start} + i} FrameSize_j \right) - Buff_{init}}{i} \right)$$

- $MaxBW_i$ be the maximum average bandwidth sustainable from the beginning of the run to the *i*th frame that does not overflow the buffer. This can be defined as

$$MaxBw_i = \min_{1 \le j \le i} \left(FrameAve_j + \frac{BufferSize}{j} \right)$$

Then, the critical bandwidth for a run is defined as a set of k frames such that the following holds for all frames within the run:

$$\max_{1 \leq j \leq k} FrameAve_j \leq MaxBW_k$$

and such that

$$\max_{1 \leq j \leq k+1} FrameAve_j > MaxBW_{k+1} .$$

The critical bandwidth for the run is the

$$CB = \max_{1 \leq j \leq k} FrameAve_j .$$

To calculate the critical bandwidth plan, we start with the first frame with no initial buffer and then calculate the critical bandwidth for the first run. If the critical point for the first run is along $F_{under}(i)$, then a decrease in bandwidth will be necessary or the buffer will eventually overflow. The next run is then started at the critical point with initial buffer 0. If the critical point for the first run is along $F_{over}(i)$, then a bandwidth increase will be necessary in the next run. As described earlier, a search is then performed at the end of the run for a starting point that maximizes the point reached by the next run. Note that this search involves a fairly trivial calculation to find the appropriate initial buffer for the next run.

3.3.4 An Optimal Bandwidth Allocation Algorithm

As shown in the last section, it is possible to minimize the total number of bandwidth increases for the continuous playback of video. The CBA plans, however, may require many adjustments that decrease the bandwidth requirement. For networks that place a premium on interacting as little with the clients as possible, the CBA can be extended to have all the properties from Theorem 2 while also minimizing the total number of bandwidth changes required. The *optimal bandwidth allocation* (OBA) algorithm results in the same number of increases in bandwidth, the same smallest peak bandwidth, and the same largest minimum bandwidth as the CBA algorithm with a maximum buffer constraint. The OBA algorithm differs from the CBA algorithm by not returning bandwidth to the network as soon as it has passed the critical point that required the bandwidth. Instead, the OBA algorithm may hold the bandwidth past the critical point in order to reduce the number of decreases in bandwidth required from the network. As a result of this, the OBA algorithm has very few changes in bandwidth for a moderately sized buffer. In the rest of this section, we motivate and describe an optimal bandwidth allocation strategy. We continue to use the definitions of critical bandwidths and critical points stated in the last section.

For our geometric model, the OBA algorithm allocates runs by performing a search on the frontier of each run such that the critical point for the next run is maximized.

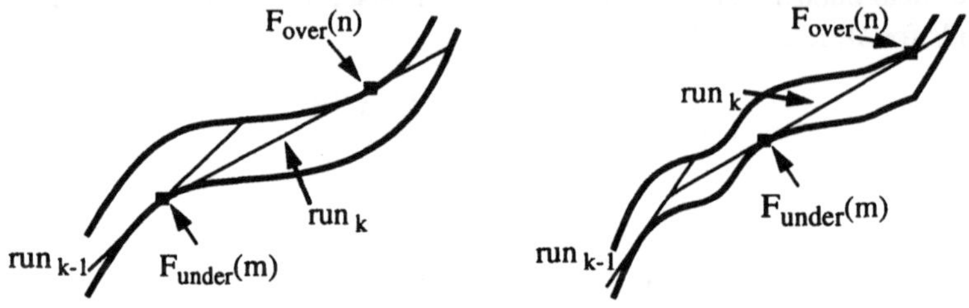

Figure 3.12: Bandwidth Search Example. This figure shows the two representative cases that may result for run *k* in which a bandwidth increase will be required in run *k+1*.

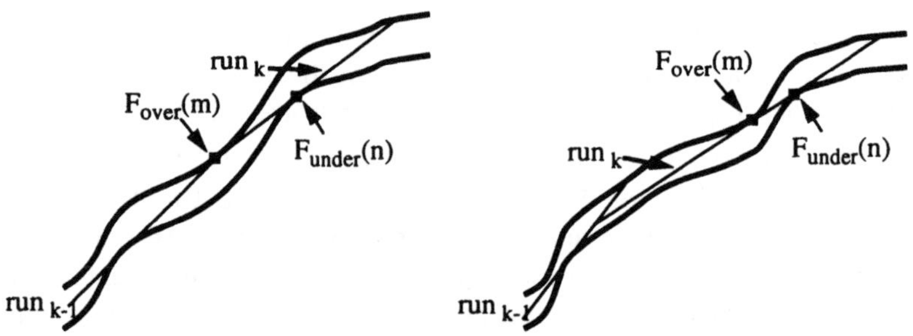

Figure 3.13: Bandwidth Search Example. This figure shows the two representative cases that arise when the search for run *k* results in another bandwidth decrease required in run *k+1*. In (a), $F_{over}(m)$ lies on the line created by run_{k-1}. In (b), $F_{over}(m)$ does not lie on run *k-1*.

As a result, the OBA algorithm attempts to allocate runs such that each run maximizes the point reachable. At the end of a particular line (run), there are two possibilities for the next run, either increase or decrease the bandwidth requirement. For our discussion, we ignore a run which can reach the end of the movie. The actual bandwidth used for the last run can be chosen so that it fall within the range of bandwidth allocations already used, or it can be chosen in such a way as to minimize the bandwidth or minimize the allocation time of the channel.

For runs which require a bandwidth increase in the next run, the same search is performed as in the CBA algorithm, resulting in a search on a line connecting $F_{over}(m)$ and $F_{under}(n)$ with $m < n$ (see Figure 3.7 and Figure 3.8). For a run which requires a bandwidth decrease in the next run, a search on the frontier of the current run results in four other possible outcomes. These representative outcomes, which are essentially mirror images of the 4 bandwidth increase cases, are shown in Figure 3.12 and Figure 3.13. Thus, for a run *k* which decreases the bandwidth from the last run, a search along a line that touches $F_{under}(m)$ and $F_{over}(n)$, with $m < n$ is performed to find a starting point for the next run that maximizes the point reachable for run *k*. This

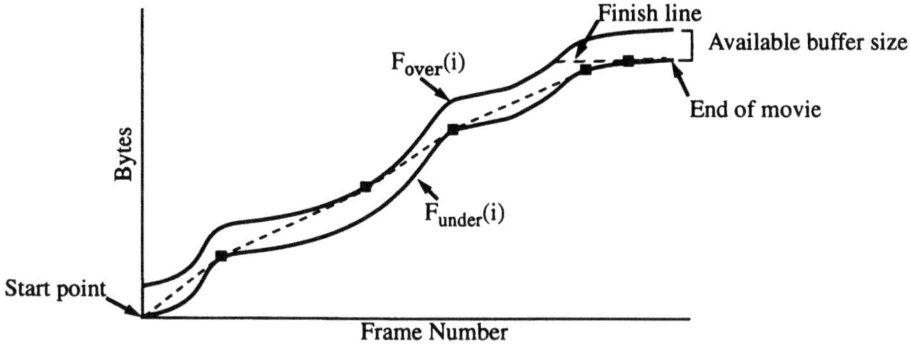

Figure 3.14: Critical Bandwidth Allocation with Maximum Buffer Example. This figure shows a sample construction of the CBA algorithm with a maximum buffer constraint. The dotted lines represent the runs within the bandwidth plan.

new line segment maximizes the critical point for the next run, while providing a transition from the last run to the current run. This leads to two more properties that are parallel to Property 1 and Property 2:

Property 3 : For a run k which (1) decreases the bandwidth requirement over run k-1 and (2) requires an increase in bandwidth in run k+1, the search for run k results in a run which is determined by the slope between the points $F_{under}(m)$ and $F_{over}(n)$ where m < n.

This property essentially says that the search for run *k* as shown in Figure 3.12, which results in a bandwidth increase in run *k+1*, is defined by two points, one from $F_{under}(i)$ and the other from $F_{over}(i)$. In addition, because run *k+1* requires an increase in bandwidth, the frontier of run *k* must end on a point on $F_{under}(i)$.

Property 4 : For a run k which (1) decreases the bandwidth requirement over run k-1 and (2) requires an decrease in bandwidth in run k+1, the search for run k results in a run which is determined by a slope between the points $F_{over}(m)$ and $F_{under}(n)$, where m < n.

This property is the similar result for bandwidth decreases. That is, the search in run *k* is defined by two points, one from $F_{over}(i)$ and the other from $F_{under}(i)$. See Figure 3.13. A sample construction is shown in Figure 3.15. Using this "greedy" approach in the allocation of each run within the OBA plan results in the following theorem:

Theorem 3 : For video playback allocation plans using a fixed size buffer, for which (a) the bytes deliverable are equal to the aggregate size of the video clip and (b) where prefetching at the start of the movie are disallowed, the optimal critical

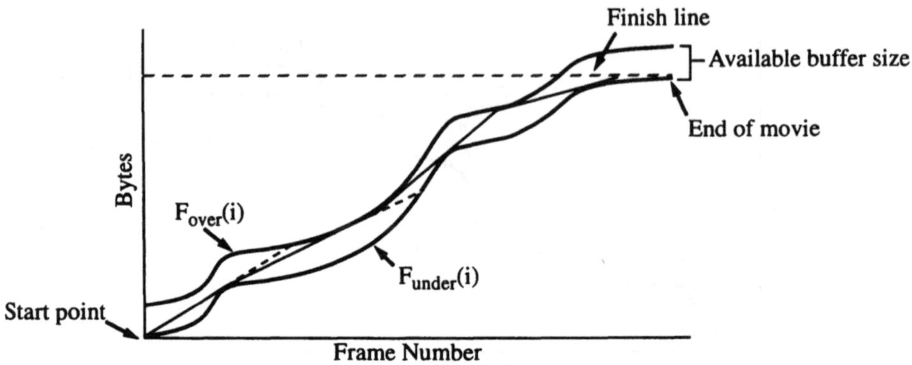

Figure 3.15: Optimal Bandwidth Allocation Construction Example. This figure shows a sample construction of the optimal bandwidth allocation algorithm. Note, this plan includes only 4 runs while the plan in Figure 3.9 required 6 runs. The heavy solid lines show $F_{over}(i)$ and $F_{under}(i)$, while the light solid lines show the slopes (bandwidths) selected by the optimal critical bandwidth allocation algorithm. The dotted lines show the lines along which the searches were performed to maximize the critical points of the following runs.

bandwidth algorithm results in (1) smallest peak bandwidth, (2) the largest minimum bandwidth, and (3) the fewest possible bandwidth changes.

Proof: To prove this theorem, we use the notation

[*inc, inc*] - for a run which increases the bandwidth from the last run and requires an increase in bandwidth in the next run

[*inc, dec*] - for a run which increases the bandwidth from the last run and requires a decrease in bandwidth in the next run

[*dec, inc*] - for a run which decreases the bandwidth from the last run and requires an increase in bandwidth in the next run

[*dec, dec*] - for a run which decreases the bandwidth from the last run and requires a decrease in bandwidth in the next run

To prove part 1 of the theorem (smallest peak bandwidth), let us consider all of the [*inc, dec*] runs within the OBA plan. Let the [*inc, dec*] run be run *i.* By Property 2, run *i* is determined by a hub that runs from $F_{hi}(m)$ to $F_{low}(n)$ for some $m < n$. We then note that any other plan that is not co-linear with run *i*, must have a run that crosses the hub of run *i.* Because this slope must be greater than that from $F_{hi}(m)$ to $F_{low}(n)$ in order to cross it, no other run can have a smaller bandwidth requirement that crosses the hub of run *i.*

To prove part 2 of the theorem, the mirror of part 1 is used. Let us consider all of the [*dec, inc*] runs within the OBA plan. Let the [*dec, inc*] run be run *i.* By Property 3, run *i* is determined by a hub that runs from $F_{low}(m)$ to $F_{hi}(n)$ for some m < n. We then note that any other plan that is not co-linear with run *i,* must have a run that crosses the hub of run *i.* Because this slope must be smaller than that from $F_{low}(m)$ to $F_{hi}(n)$ in order to cross it, no other run can have a larger bandwidth requirement that crosses the hub of run *i.*

To prove part 3 of the theorem, we show by contradiction that the OBA algorithm results in the minimum number of bandwidth changes. Suppose the OBA algorithm creates a bandwidth plan, $plan_{opt}$, that has *X* bandwidth changes in it. Further, suppose that his plan is not optimal in the number of bandwidth changes. Therefore, another plan, $plan_{better}$, must exist that has *fewer* than *X* bandwidth changes in it. As a result, there must exist at least one run in $plan_{better}$ that spans greater than one run from $plan_{opt}$. As will be shown, this cannot happen.

For algorithms that do not allow prefetching, both bandwidth plans must start on the first frame and have nothing in the smoothing buffer. As a result, $plan_{opt}$, whether it requires an increase or decrease in bandwidth in the next run, will result in a plan that has a critical point greater than or equal to the first run in $plan_{better}$. If an increase in bandwidth is required in the next run, $plan_{opt}$ picks the bandwidth such that any more bandwidth would result in buffer overflow. Any bandwidth higher results in buffer overflow before the critical point of the first run in $plan_{opt}$. Any less bandwidth results in a critical point that is before the critical point of the first run in $plan_{opt}$. If a decrease in bandwidth is required in the next run, then by definition, $plan_{opt}$ has chosen the minimal bandwidth necessary without overflow resulting in the furthest critical point possible. Thus, $plan_{better}$ cannot have a critical point that is further out than $plan_{opt}$ for the first run, and hence, cannot cross the frontier of the first run in $plan_{opt}$ in the first run.

For each run after the first run, $plan_{opt}$ starts by examining the frontier of the last run and finds a starting frame that will maximize the critical point of the current run. This search is always performed a line connecting $F_{low}(i)$ and $F_{hi}(i)$ OR $F_{hi}(i)$ and $F_{low}(i)$. Because this search is on a line that connects F_{hi} and F_{low} which $plan_{better}$ must cross, $plan_{better}$ cannot pick a next run that is longer than the one chosen by $plan_{opt}$. Otherwise, $plan_{opt}$ would have found it in its search. We continue this process for all runs within the $plan_{opt}$. Because every *i*th run in $plan_{better}$ cannot have a critical point further than the *i*th run in $plan_{opt}$, $plan_{better}$ must have at least as many runs as $plan_{opt}$. Therefore, $plan_{opt}$ results in the fewest number of bandwidth changes.//

OBA Implementation

To construct the optimal bandwidth allocation plan, we use the same algorithm for finding the critical bandwidth and critical point for a run as defined in Section 3.3.3. The OBA plan then consists of three types of allocations: the beginning run, a run that decreases the bandwidth allocation, and a run that increases the bandwidth allocation.

The beginning run does not have any prefetch in order to minimize the latency between channel set-up and the beginning of playback. Therefore, the first run, is set to the critical bandwidth and critical point for the run starting at the beginning of the movie with an initial buffer of 0. Next, if the critical point for the run lies on $F_{under}(i)$ a bandwidth decrease is required in the second run. If the critical point for the run lies on $F_{over}(i)$ a bandwidth increase is required in the second run.

In the calculation of a run that decreases the bandwidth allocation, a search on the frontier of the previous run is performed to determine how far the bandwidth should be held past the end of the previous run's critical point (See Figure 3.12 and Figure 3.13). The search finds a frame, *j*, such that using the same bandwidth allocation from the end of the last run results in the critical point in the current run to be as far out as possible. The bandwidth for the run is then set to the critical bandwidth of the last run up to, and including, frame *j*, while the bandwidth from frame *j+1* to the critical point is set to the critical bandwidth for the run starting on frame *j+1*, with the appropriate initial buffer.

In the calculation for a run that increases the bandwidth allocation, a search on the frontier of the previous run is performed to find a frame, *k*, such that the current run extends as far into time as possible. The current run is then started on frame *k* and has its bandwidth allocation set to the critical bandwidth starting from frame *k* with its critical point determining the end of the run.

For each subsequent run, we apply the same algorithm to determine which of the calculations to use (whether for increasing or decreasing the bandwidth). A sample allocation plan is shown in Figure 3.10.

3.4 Evaluation of Algorithms

From the point of view of network management, load estimation, the necessary bandwidth resources, and admission control are crucial to providing guarantees of service. These can be greatly simplified if all channels exhibit constant behavior. In the absence of an entirely constant bandwidth allocation, a network manager can handle the partitioning of its bandwidth in several ways. The network manager can reserve the bandwidth at the expected peak bandwidth requirement for the channel, in which case, minimizing the peak bandwidth is important. The network manager can also let the clients allocate bandwidth as they go along, if it does not have provisions for in-advance bandwidth reservations. In this case, both the number and magnitude of

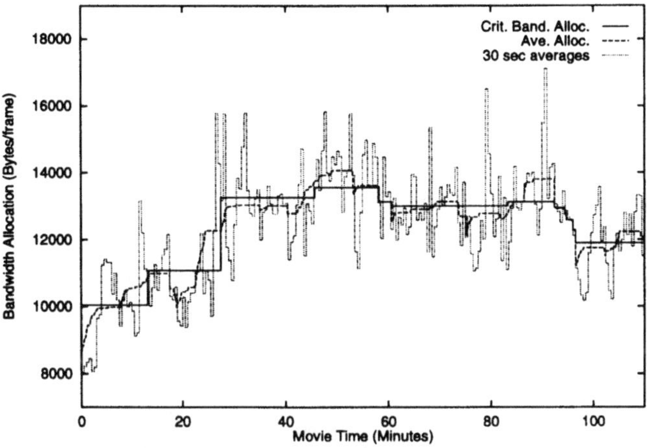

Figure 3.16: Comparison of Bandwidth Allocation Algorithms. This graph shows the results of smoothing using the average allocation based and CBA algorithm with a 10 MByte buffer for smoothing. The data above was obtained by using the movie *Speed.* Because the sliding window smoothing algorithm has two possible parameters, chunk size and window size, we fixed the chunk size at 90 frames and expanded the window to take advantage of the buffer (in this case 81 chunk window size).

bandwidth increases can be important because the bandwidth increase requests may be denied. As a result, three measures that influence this performance are the frequency of requests for increased bandwidth, the size of these increases, and the peak bandwidth requirements. The frequency and size of decreases can be interesting as well if the network management makes some provision for lowering a bandwidth reservation. We break the evaluation of the algorithms presented in this chapter into two parts. We first compare and contrast the window-based smoothing algorithms with the CBA algorithms. We then move into a more in-depth comparison of the various critical bandwidth allocation based techniques.

3.4.1 Averaging Techniques Versus CBA

To test the effectiveness of the window-based algorithms and the CBA algorithm, each algorithm was run on the digitized movie *Speed.* Figure 3.16 shows the results of smoothing using a 10 MByte buffer. This graph shows that the critical bandwidth approach produces smooth allocation with infrequent adjustments in bandwidth, requiring only 4 negotiations for increased bandwidth. It is interesting to note that the critical bandwidth algorithm require increases only after large valleys of small frame sizes. While the sliding window smoothing technique reduced the peak bandwidth requirements, it still requires the network to incrementally give bandwidth to it as a burst of large frame sizes approaches. Figure 3.17 shows the buffer utilization for the sliding window smoothing algorithm and the critical bandwidth allocation algorithm.

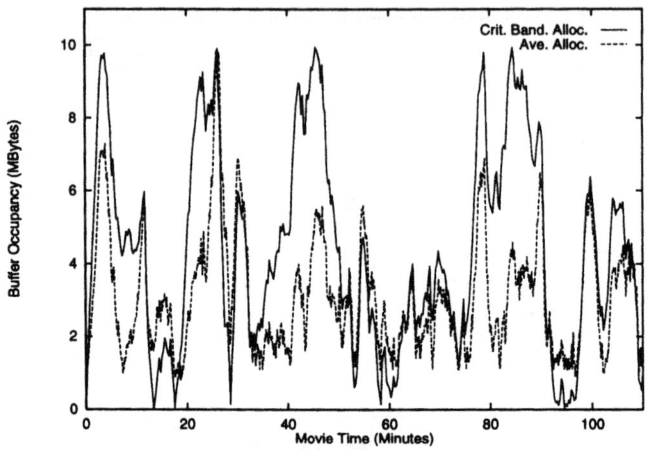

Figure 3.17: Comparison of Bandwidth Allocation Algorithms. This graph shows the utilization of a 10 Mbyte buffer for the sliding window smoothing and the CBA algorithms. The size of the sliding window is a constant, set in such a way as to make use of the full buffer in the worst case. However, the algorithm is only able to use the buffer in the first part of the video clip. A larger window in the second half of the segment would have taken better advantage of the buffer. The CBA algorithm adjusts its bandwidth to take full advantage of the buffer.

As shown by the figure, the critical bandwidth algorithm results in the buffer reaching near capacity several times, while the smoothing window sliding algorithm is set in such a way as to make use of the full buffer in the worst case. In fact, the critical bandwidth allocation algorithm results in a full buffer at least once for each increase in bandwidth that occurs within the video. The sliding window smoothing algorithm, on the other hand, would benefit from a larger window in the second half of the movie.

To avoid overtaxing network resources, bandwidth allocations have to be tracked and approved by some network manager. Increases in bandwidth are particularly important because they may be denied and some adjustment will have to be made, such as a change in quality of service, the establishment of an alternative route, or perhaps the allocation of additional prefetch buffer space.

Increases in Bandwidth

In Figure 3.18, the total number of bandwidth increases is shown as a function of buffer size. The sliding window algorithms makes many small bandwidth increase requests. This stems from the fact that when a large burst of frames first moves into the sliding window, the window size limits the amount of smoothing that can be done. Consequently, as the burst continues to move through the window it is smoothed across many groups, requiring bandwidth increases every 1 to 2 seconds. The average allocation algorithm uses larger chunks for an equivalent buffer size and therefore

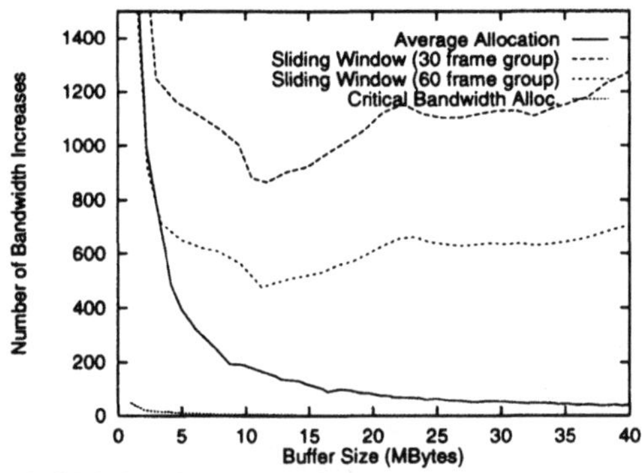

Figure 3.18: Bandwidth Increase Requests. This graph shows the total number of bandwidth increase requests for the 110-minute length movie *Speed.* The average allocation algorithm varied the chunk size in order to make use of the extra buffer space. The sliding window algorithms chunk sizes were fixed at 30 and 60 frame chunks and then the window size was varied to obtain the amount of smoothing given some buffer space. The CBA algorithm used the buffer size to determine the bandwidth requests.

calls for fewer increases in bandwidth than does the sliding window algorithm. Because the smoothing is still limited by the size of the period used, the average allocation algorithm requires substantially more increases in bandwidth. The critical bandwidth algorithm makes a low number of increase requests as expected. As an example, with a 12 MByte buffer, the critical bandwidth algorithm requires only 3 (including the initial bandwidth request) increases in the bandwidth allocation. As a result, increases occur on average of every 36 minutes. With a 14 Mbyte buffer only 2 increases are needed (one in the beginning of the movie) and one in the middle.

The size of a requested increase can be important, since the larger the increase, the less likely the network manager will have sufficient bandwidth available. Critical bandwidth allocation makes adjustments that are larger on average than does sliding window smoothing. However, this is often because sliding window smoothing will break a large change in bandwidth into a number of requests. It is, therefore, useful to examine the total size of increases requested from the different algorithms.

As Figure 3.19 shows, the average allocation algorithm makes the worst use of buffer space, requiring large changes in the actual bandwidth allocation requirements. The primary limitation of this algorithm lies in its inability to effectively prefetch data. The only way for the algorithm to obtain a lower increase cost was to increase the size of the chunks. By using the sliding window smoother, the size of the chunk can remain relatively small, reducing the amount of buffer space used to store the next chunk. By using this extra buffer space to prefetch bursts of large frames, the sliding-window algorithms are more effective in smoothing bandwidth curves than the average allocation algorithm. The critical bandwidth algorithm has the smallest cost

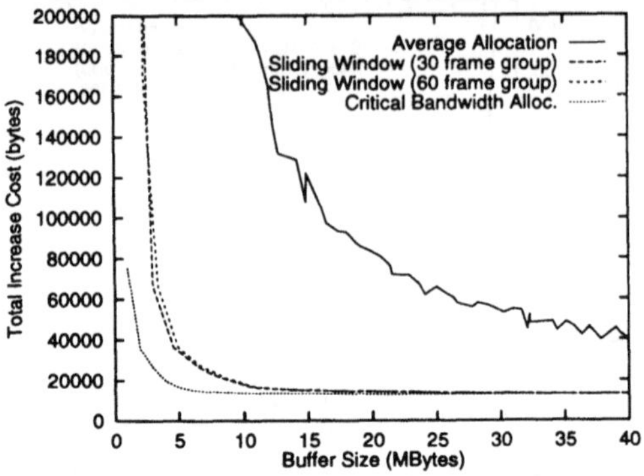

Figure 3.19: Bandwidth Increase Costs. The total increase cost of each algorithm is the summation of all bandwidth *increase* requests for the movie *Speed.* While both sliding window smoothing and critical bandwidth allocation lead to a small cost for large buffers, sliding window allocation spreads its increases over a much greater number of requests.

because it minimizes the total range of bandwidth requirements as well as the number of bandwidth increases required within that range.

Decreases in Bandwidth

A decrease in required bandwidth may require an interaction with the network manager, but will not be disallowed due to contention for resources. Some approaches to access control assume that bandwidths will be constant, but smoothing shows that within lengthy segments it may be monotonically decreasing. Thus, there may be benefits in developing admission control policies that allow reserved bandwidth to be released without terminating a channel. The critical bandwidth algorithm does a good job of identifying blocks of bandwidth that can be released in a low number of requests (see Figure 3.20).

Peak Bandwidth Requirement

For systems that allocate bandwidth based on the peak bandwidth requirements, minimizing the peak bandwidth used as well as the range of bandwidths used can be helpful with admission control. As shown in Figure 3.21, the average allocation algorithm does not always lower the peak bandwidth requirement given more buffer for smoothing. The primary limitation is that the averaging algorithm can only use larger and larger period sizes to accomplish more smoothing, hence, the boundaries for the calculation of averages continue to change as more buffer is added. Fixing the period size and then increasing the window size has the effect of smoothing the bandwidth requirements as more buffer is added. As more buffer is added, the additional buffer is used strictly for prefetching bursts of data in the future. The critical bandwidth algorithm finds the minimum peak and maximum valley bandwidths. For buffers greater than 17 MBytes, the first run determined the maximum bandwidth requirement for the

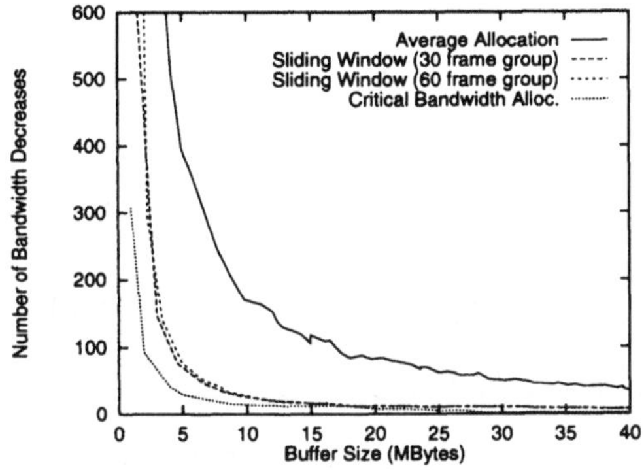

Figure 3.20: Bandwidth Decrease Requests. This graph shows the total number of bandwidth decrease requests for the movie *Speed.* The CBA algorithm makes more decrease requests than increase requests. The sliding window smoothing algorithm on the other hand, makes many fewer requests to decrease bandwidth than to increase, since increases are frequently spread across several requests.

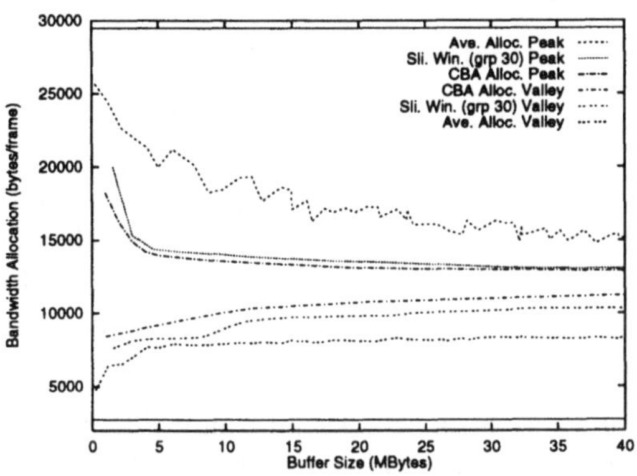

Figure 3.21: Bandwidth Requirement Ranges. This graph shows the bandwidth requirements ranges for the movie *Speed.* The solid horizontal lines are the minimum and maximum frame sizes for the movie.

movie. If prefetching is allowed (and the delay is tolerable), the peak bandwidth requirement for buffers greater than 17 MBytes can be reduced further.

3.4.2 Non-Window Based Smoothing Algorithms

In this section, we compare and contrast the various critical bandwidth based algorithms. To highlight how the video data affects the amount of smoothing available, we have graphed the bandwidth allocation plans for the OBA algorithm using both a 10 and 30 MByte buffer for several of the movies in the video library in Figure 3.34 through Figure 3.38 at the end of the chapter. Graphs for all the movies using the OBA algorithm can be found in [FENG96b]

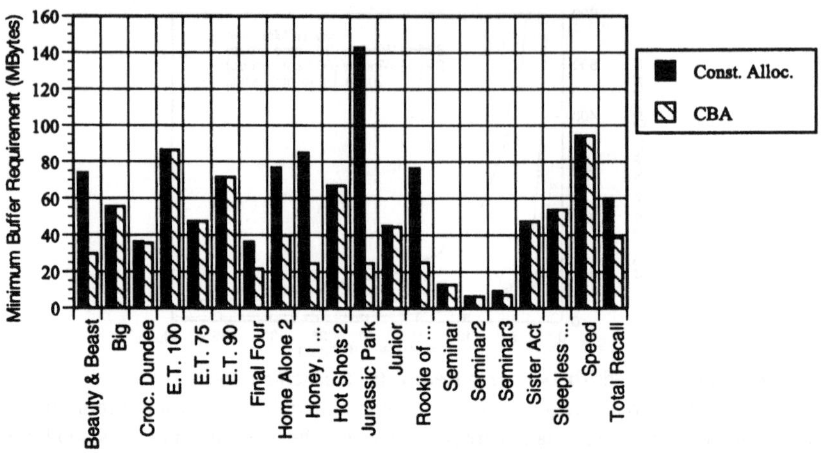

Figure 3.22: Critical Bandwidth Allocation Minimum Buffer Requirement. This figure shows the maximum buffer requirements for the movies encoded using the CBA algorithm with no buffer limitation.

Critical Bandwidth Allocation without Buffer Constraint

When sufficient buffering is available, allocating the bandwidth using the critical bandwidth algorithm without a buffer constraint is useful because admission control becomes trivial. The admission control algorithm simply sees if there is enough bandwidth to start the flow of data. Recall that the critical bandwidth algorithm results in a monotonically decreasing sequence of bandwidth allocations. In addition, the playback of the video can start once the video has been accepted to the network.

In Figure 3.22, we have graphed the amount of buffer required to play back the captured video clips using both a single constant bandwidth allocation (chosen to minimize the buffer used) and the critical bandwidth allocation algorithm. As shown by this figure, several of the movies have the same constant allocation and CBA minimum buffer size requirements (E.g. *E.T.* and *Hot Shots 2*). In these clips, the constant bandwidth allocation plan is determined by two points on $F_{under}()$, where the maximum buffer requirement occurs between these two points. For other clips, the CBA plan requires smaller amounts of buffer than the single constant bandwidth allocation plan (E.g. *Beauty and the Beast* and *Jurassic Park*). Of particular interest is the *Jurassic Park* video, which requires almost 8 times as much buffer space to playback than the CBA plan. This is mainly due to the fact that *Jurassic Park* has larger frames (on average) for the first half of the movie and smaller frames on average for the second half. As a result, during the second half of the movie, the buffer continues to build using a single constant allocation, while the CBA algorithm reduces the bandwidth allocation to avoid a large build-up in buffer. Finally, the constant bandwidth allocation plans also require prefetch delay, while the CBA plans allow the playback to begin once the first frame of the bandwidth plan has been received.

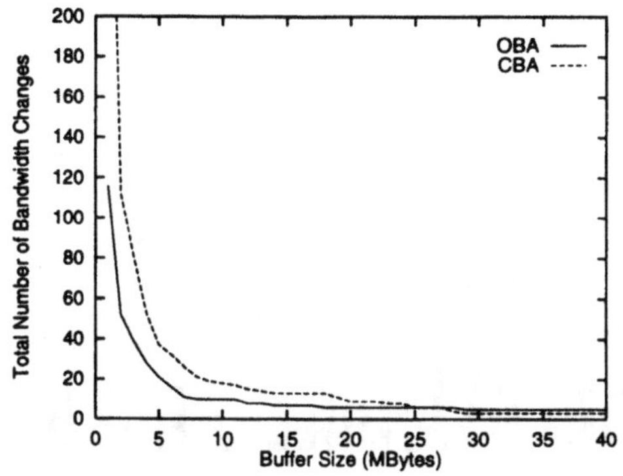

Figure 3.23: Bandwidth Change Requests. The graphs above show the total number of required bandwidth allocation change requests for the movie *Speed.*

For the CBA plan, the total amount of buffering depends primarily on two factors, the average size of the frames and the long-term burstiness of the video. If the movie had a sustained area of smaller frames followed by a sustained area of larger frames, the amount of buffering tended to be much higher. As examples, the seminar videos required much smaller buffer sizes because both the size and variation of frames sizes were small in these videos. The *E.T.* videos required proportionately larger buffers as the quality was increased. Because these videos exhibited the same long term burstiness, the differences are due mostly to the increase in the frame sizes within the videos. Just the average size of frames, however, is not indicative of the minimum buffer requirements. The movie *Speed* required a larger buffer than the *E.T.* (Quality 100) video even though both the variance in frame sizes and the average frame sizes were smaller in the *Speed* video. Thus, the buffer size is primarily due to the long term burstiness, and to a lesser degree, the average frame sizes within the videos. One final note on the video data; using MPEG video data rather than MJPEG data can typically result in buffer requirements that are approximately 4-7 times smaller, assuming that the MPEG movie contains P and B frames.

Bandwidth Changes

As Figure 3.23 shows, the OBA algorithm results in a fewer number of bandwidth changes than the CBA algorithm for a given buffer size, as expected. As an example, using the *Speed* video, a 5 MByte smoothing buffer, and the OBA algorithm results in 21 bandwidth changes over the 110 minute movie, while the critical bandwidth algorithm requires 37 changes in bandwidth. On average the optimal bandwidth allocation algorithm requires a bandwidth change approximately every 5 minutes, using only 5 MBytes of buffer. After the initial start of the movie, the *Speed* movie using the OBA algorithm had a minimum run length of approximately 1 minute and 45 seconds and a maximum run length of approximately 14 minutes. By using a 10 MByte buffer for buffering, the shortest and longest run lengths grow to 13 minutes and 25.5 minutes,

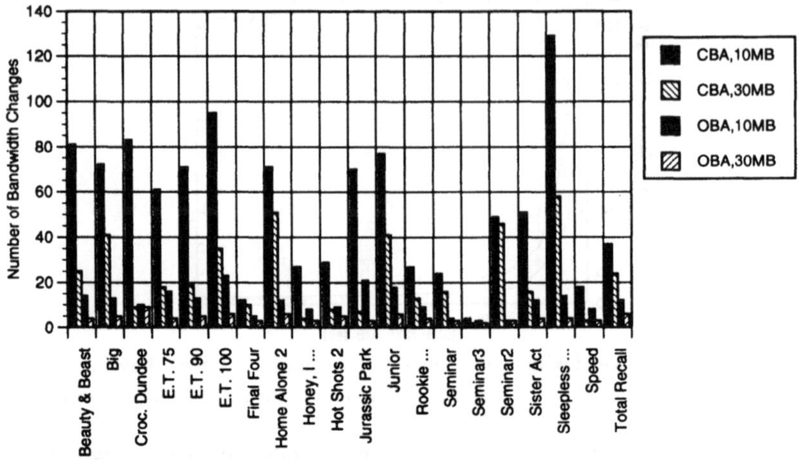

Figure 3.24: Bandwidth Changes for All Movies. This graph show the number of bandwidth changes required for all of the sample movies using a 10 and 30 MB buffer and the OBA and CBA Algorithms.

respectively. As a result, a moderate amount of buffering can reduce the number of interactions required from the network to the order of tens of minutes.

As shown in Figure 3.24, the total number of bandwidth changes required is relatively small even for a 10 MByte buffer with loosely encoded video. The OBA algorithm results in a large difference in required bandwidth changes. For a 10 MByte smoothing buffer, the movie *E.T.* (Quality 100) requires 23 bandwidth changes with the OBA algorithm, which is the maximum number of changes required for all the movies using the OBA algorithm. On average, the OBA algorithm results in 73% fewer bandwidth changes than the CBA algorithm for a 10 MByte smoothing buffer and 63% fewer bandwidth changes at 30 MBytes. The distinction between increases and decreases in the bandwidth allocation plan can be useful because the requests for decreases in bandwidth can generally be satisfied, while increases may require further negotiations with the network. In addition, it highlights the main differences between the various algorithms.

Bandwidth Decrease Requests

As shown in Figure 3.25, the total number of bandwidth decreases for the *Speed* video are similar to the total number of bandwidth change graph (Figure 3.23). This is not entirely unexpected because the CBA and OBA algorithms result in the minimum number of bandwidth increases necessary for continuous playback. Thus, a large percentage of the bandwidth changes are due to decreases in bandwidth, which from a network point of view should be easier to satisfy. In comparing the optimal bandwidth algorithm with the critical bandwidth algorithm, we see that the main difference between these algorithms is in the number of bandwidth decreases (as shown by the

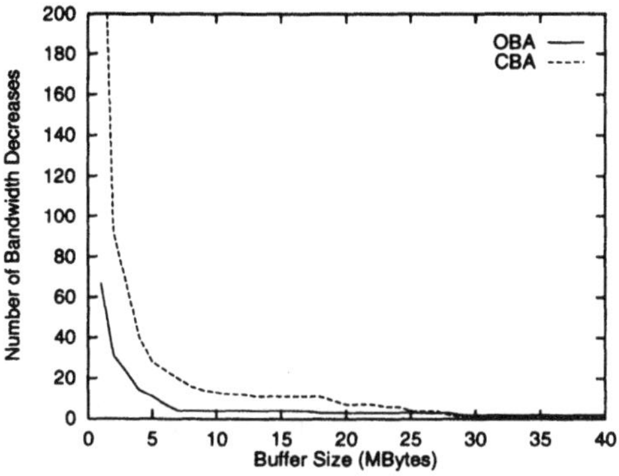

Figure 3.25: Bandwidth Decrease Requests. The graphs above show the total number of bandwidth allocation decrease requests for the movie *Speed*.

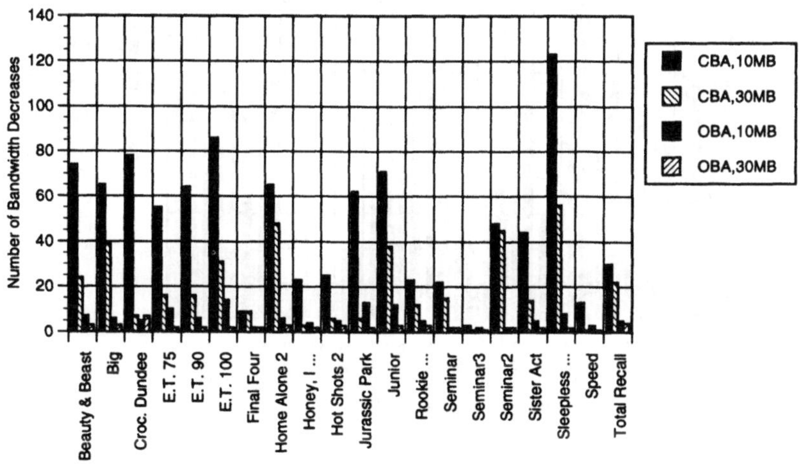

Figure 3.26: Bandwidth Decreases for All Movies. This graph show the number of bandwidth decreases required by the OBA and CBA algorithms for 10 and 30 MB buffers for all the sample movies.

same relative differences in total bandwidth changes and total number of decreases). The critical bandwidth allocation algorithm allocates each run at the minimum bandwidth requirement to avoid underflow, while the optimal bandwidth starts each run at the minimum bandwidth requirement but holds the bandwidth past the critical point of the run to prefetch data for the next run.

Bandwidth Increase Requests

For bandwidth increases, using the CBA and OBA algorithms result in the same number of increases across all buffer size constraints for each movie, therefore, verifying Theorem 2. As shown in Figure 3.27, the number of increases required for the movie *Speed* drops to 5 increases for buffers greater than 8 MBytes and drops to only 2

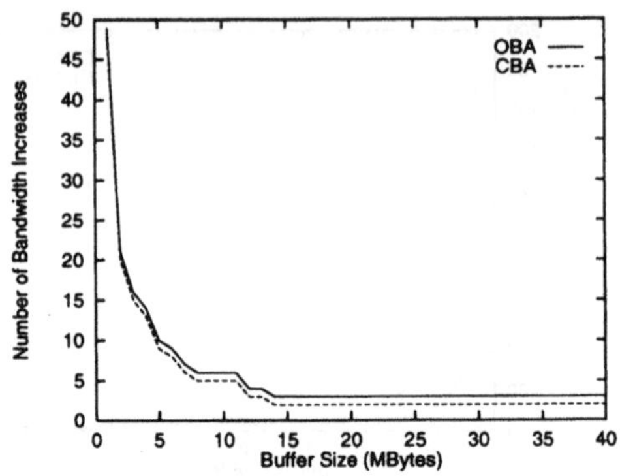

Figure 3.27: Bandwidth Increase Requests. The graph above shows the total number of bandwidth allocation increase requests for the movie *Speed.*

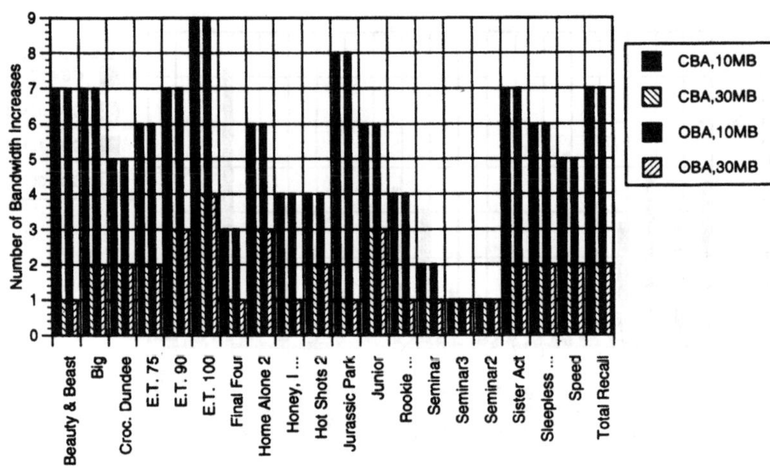

Figure 3.28: Bandwidth Increases for All Movies. This graph shows the number of bandwidth increases required using the OBA and CBA algorithms with a 10MB and 30 MB buffer.

increases for buffers greater than 14 MBytes. As a result, interactions with the network will only be required, on average, every 21 and 55 minutes for an 8 and 14 Mbyte smoothing buffer, respectively. As shown in Figure 3.28, all the other movies exhibited similar behavior to the *Speed* video. It is interesting to note that all but 4 of the videos require only one increase in the bandwidth requirement after the initial bandwidth allocation.

Bandwidth Increase Magnitude

Requests for increases in bandwidth allocation require interaction with the network manager for more resources. The frequency and magnitude of these increases will determine the network's ability to adapt to changing network load. Comparison of

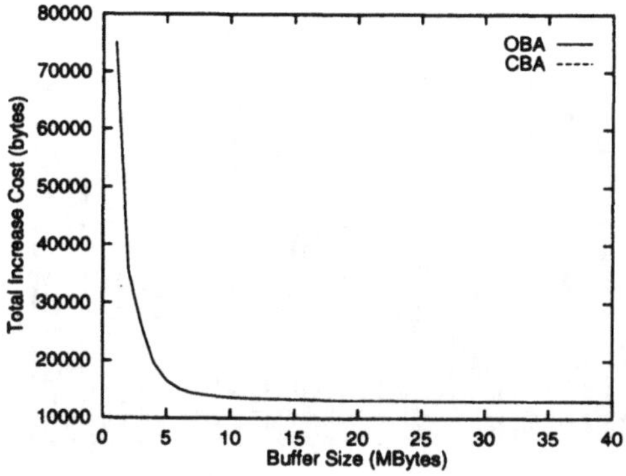

Figure 3.29: Bandwidth Increase Costs. The graph above shows the total sum (magnitude) of all the bandwidth allocation increase requests for the movie *Speed*. The CBA and OBA algorithms were applied with different buffer capacities. The optimal bandwidth allocation algorithm and the critical bandwidth allocation algorithm result in the same totals.

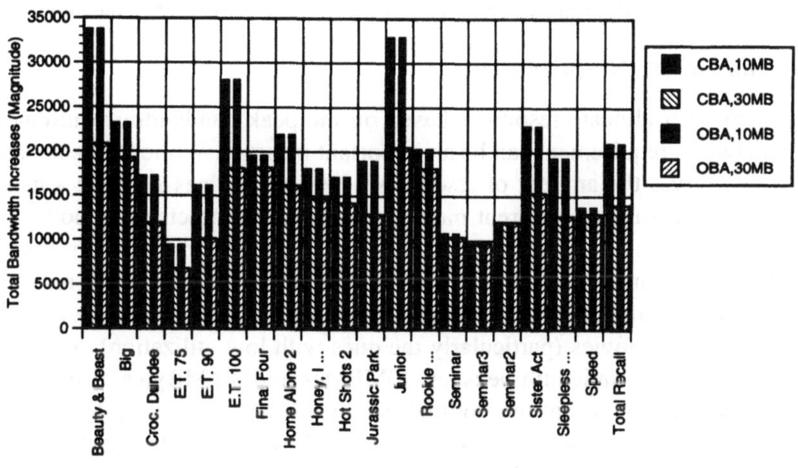

Figure 3.30: Bandwidth Increase Requests for All Movies. This figure shows the total magnitude of all the bandwidth increase requests for the sample movies using the OBA and CBA algorithms.

increases in bandwidth magnitudes are only relevant when the total number of increase requests is the same. As an example, if one stream requests 1000 bytes/frame more bandwidth and another asks for 100 bytes/frame on ten separate occasions, no comparison can be made. Because the critical bandwidth based algorithms have the same number of increases for a given movie and both have the minimum-peak and highest-minimum bandwidths, their results are the same. As shown in Figure 3.29, the critical bandwidth algorithm with prefetching and the optimal bandwidth allocation algorithm have the same total magnitude of bandwidth increases.

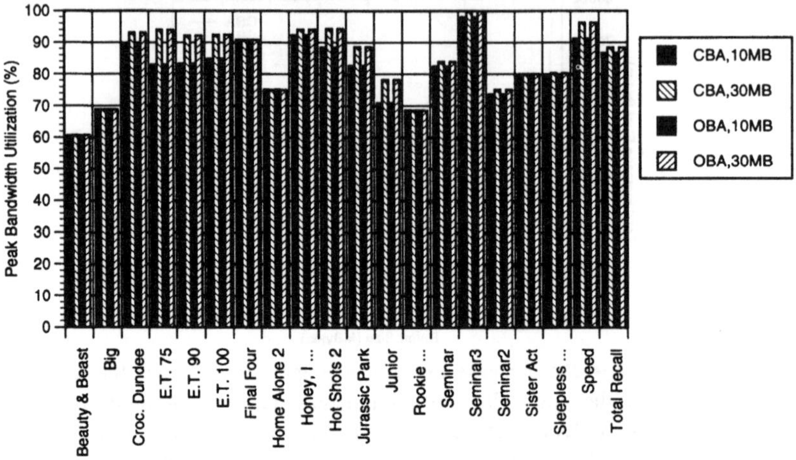

Figure 3.31: Peak Bandwidth Utilization for All Movies. This figure shows the utilization of resources allocated using the peak bandwidth requirement and the OBA and CBA algorithms (with no initial prefetching at the start of the movie).

Peak Bandwidth Requirements

For systems that allocate resources based on the peak bandwidth requirements, the peak bandwidth requirement can be an important measure. While the peak bandwidth requirement gives the amount of resources necessary, it does not give a method for comparing the results of different movies. To show the effects of smoothing on our sample movies, we have assumed that the peak bandwidth requirement are used for the entire movie and then calculate the utilization of the bandwidth reserved. The peak bandwidth utilization measurements are shown in Figure 3.31. From this graph, we see that some movies (particularly the ones with low utilization) do not improve their utilization of bandwidth between 10MBytes and 30 MBytes of buffering. The main reason for this is that the optimal bandwidth algorithm may have an initially high bandwidth requirement in order to satisfy a low latency start of the video, however, once this initially high bandwidth requirement is passed, a lower peak bandwidth requirement results for the rest of the movie. To show this, we have also graphed what we call the *tumbling utilization* measurement, which measures the utilization of the bandwidth reserved in the same way as the peak bandwidth utilization measurement with one exception. Once the peak bandwidth requirement has passed for the entire movie, the bandwidth can be reduced to the peak bandwidth for the rest of the movie. An example of the tumbling bandwidth utilization calculation is shown in Figure 3.32. As Figure 3.33 shows, the tumbling bandwidth utilizations are much higher than the peak bandwidth utilization measurements, mostly due to the initially high bandwidth requirement of the optimal bandwidth allocation plans. The movie *Junior* has the lowest utilization of all the movies. This movie has a large burst of frames at the end of the movie, resulting in the peak bandwidth requirement at the end

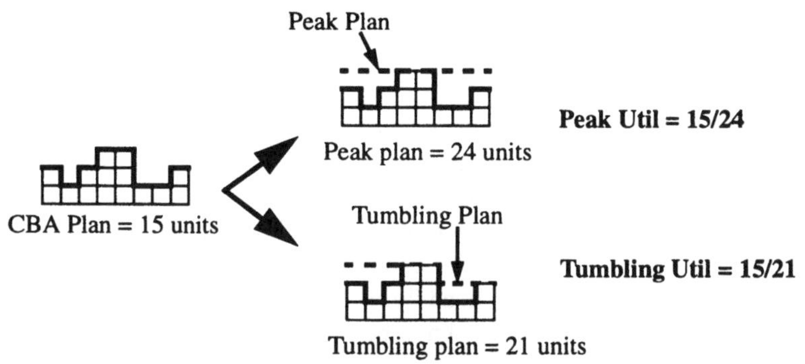

Figure 3.32: Peak Utilization vs. Tumbling Utilization. This figure shows the difference between the peak and tumbling utilization calculations. The CBA plan (heavy solid line) requires 15 units of bandwidth (represented by squares). The tumbling utilization plan always results in a utilization greater than or equal to the peak utilization.

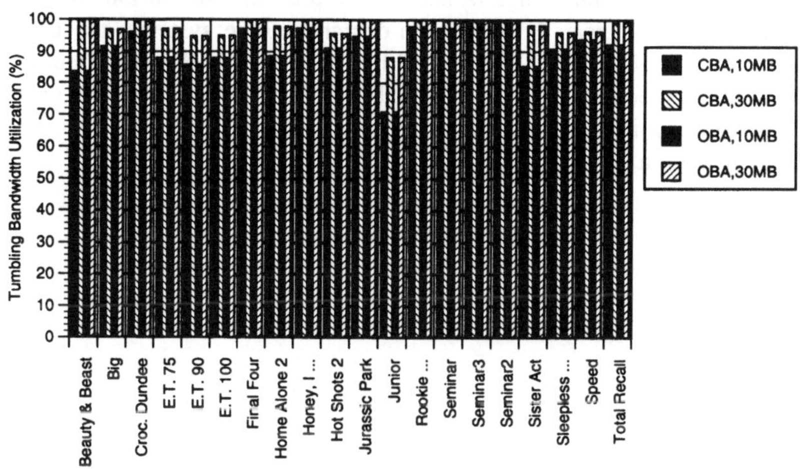

Figure 3.33: Tumbling Bandwidth Utilization for All Movies. This figure shows the tumbling utilization for the OBA and CBA algorithms on the sample movies.

of the movie, resulting in a lower utilization than exhibited by the other movies. With the exception of *Junior*, it is interesting to note that the optimal bandwidth algorithm resulted in utilizations between 94% and 100%, with 10 of the movies having greater than 99% utilization.

3.5 Summary of Bandwidth Smoothing Algorithms

In this chapter, we have examined several bandwidth smoothing algorithms that can be used for the delivery of compressed video streams. Window-based smoothing algorithms are useful in smoothing bandwidth requirements where the delay between the receipt and playback of a frame must adhere to some maximum delay. Thus, window-based smoothing algorithms are particularly suited for live-video applications.

The non-window-based *critical bandwidth allocation* algorithms have been shown to be useful for the delivery of prerecorded compressed video, where the *a priori* knowledge of the video is obtainable before the bandwidth reservations are made. The CBA-based algorithms have been shown to minimize both the peak bandwidth requirements as well as the number of bandwidth increases required for the delivery of compressed prerecorded video. In addition, we have shown that the CBA algorithm can be extended to minimize the total number of changes in bandwidth as well.

For stored video applications, the use of critical bandwidth allocation plans in admission control can help in the efficient allocation of network resources. For a system that has smaller clips such as those in an educational interactive setting, using the critical bandwidth allocation approach without a maximum buffer constraint makes admission control easier by having to perform only a single check for admission control. In addition, with smaller clips which last less than an hour, the amount of buffering needed is not as great. For video-on-demand movie systems, the use of the optimal bandwidth allocation algorithm with a maximum buffer constraint can also simplify admission control because the number of bandwidth changes as well as the peak bandwidth requirements are minimized. We will examine the use of the optimal bandwidth allocation algorithm in a general setting in the next chapter.

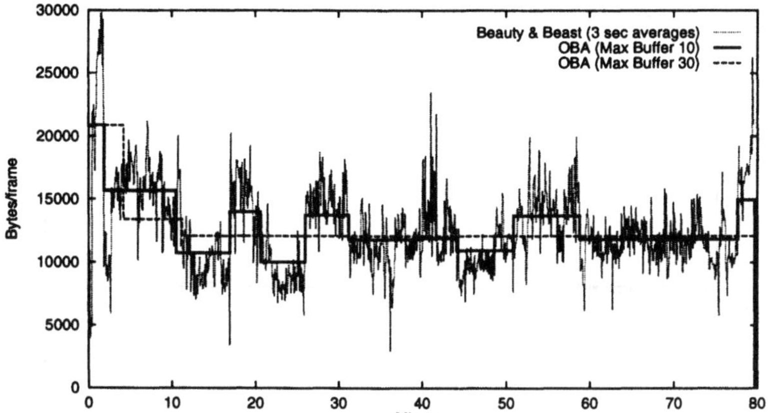

Figure 3.34: ***Beauty and the Beast*** **- OBA Example.**

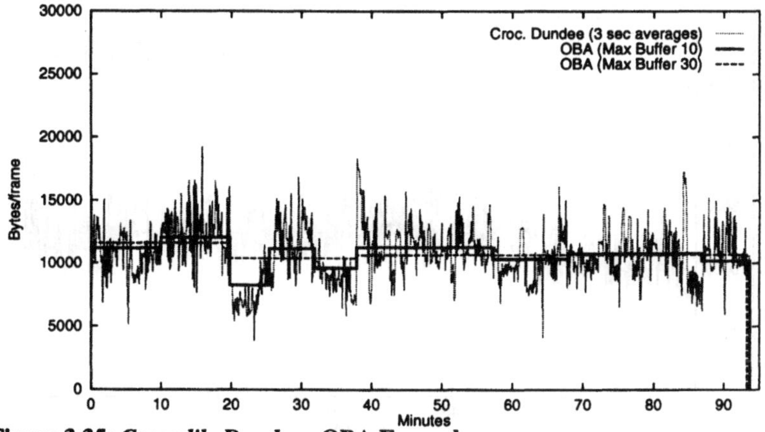

Figure 3.35: ***Crocodile Dundee*** **- OBA Example.**

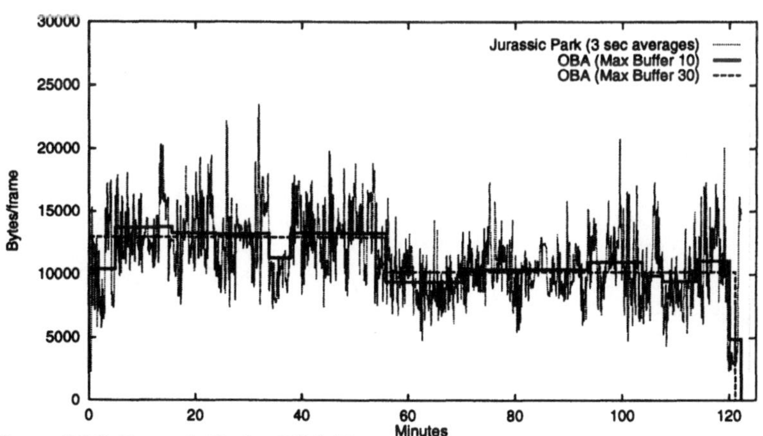

Figure 3.36: ***Jurassic Park*** **- OBA Example.**

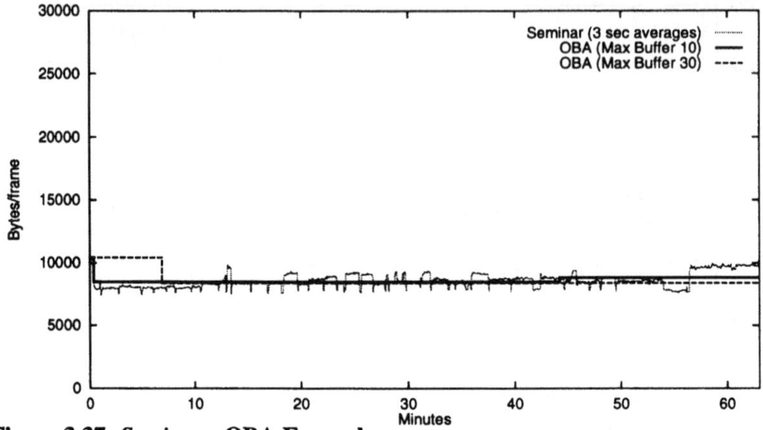

Figure 3.37: ***Seminar*** **- OBA Example.**

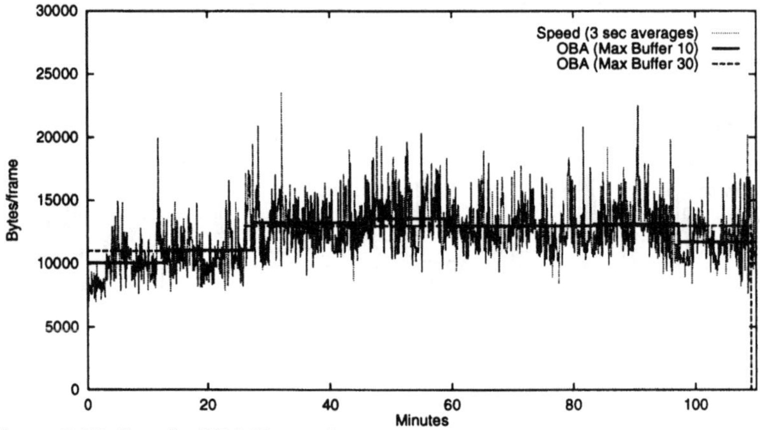

Figure 3.38: ***Speed*** **- OBA Example.**

4

A SURVEY OF BANDWIDTH SMOOTHING TECHNIQUES

4.1 Introduction

After the introduction of the critical bandwidth based smoothing techniques, several new bandwidth smoothing techniques have appeared in the literature. In this chapter, we briefly review the bandwidth smoothing techniques described in the last chapter and present the bandwidth smoothing algorithms that have since appeared in the literature. After a discussion of the various bandwidth smoothing algorithms, we contrast and compare the algorithms using several metrics, highlighting the unique properties that each algorithm exhibits.

4.2 Background

In this section, we review the bandwidth smoothing problem formulation and present the bandwidth smoothing algorithms that have appeared in the literature. We have broken the discussion of the bandwidth smoothing algorithms into those that base the bandwidth smoothing plan on both the $F_{under}()$ and $F_{over}()$ curves (Section 4.2.2) and those that create bandwidth smoothing plans based solely on the $F_{under}()$ function (Section 4.2.3).

4.2.1 Overflow and Underflow Constraints

Recall, a compressed video stream consists of n frames, where frame i requires f_i bytes of storage. To permit continuous playback at the client site, the server must always transmit quickly enough to avoid buffer underflow, where

$$F_{under}(k) = \sum_{i=0}^{k} f_i$$

indicates the amount of data consumed at the client by frame k, where $k=0,1,\ldots n-1$. Similarly, the client should not receive more data than

$$F_{over}(k) = \sum_{i=0}^{k} f_i + b$$

by frame k, to prevent overflow of the playback buffer (of size b). Consequently, any valid server transmission plan should stay within the river outlined by these vertically equidistant functions. That is,

$$F_{under}(k) \le \sum_{i=0}^{k} c_i \le F_{over}(k)$$

where c_i is the transmission rate during frame slot i of the smoothed video stream.

Creating a bandwidth plan involves generating m consecutive *runs* each with a constant bandwidth allocation r_j and a duration t_j, where time is measured in discrete frame slots; at time i the server transmits at rate $c_i=r_j$, where slot i occurs during run j. Together, the m bandwidth runs must form a monotonically-increasing, piecewise-linear path that stays between the F_{under} and F_{over} curves. Bandwidth smoothing algorithms typically select the starting point for run $j+1$ based on the trajectory for run j. By extending the fixed-rate line for run j, the trajectory eventually encounters either the underflow or the overflow curve, or both, requiring a change in the server transmission rate.

4.2.2 Smoothing Based on F_{over} and F_{under}

Several different smoothing algorithms have been introduced that use both the F_{over} and F_{under} curves in computing the bandwidth runs in the transmission plans. Given a starting point for run $j+1$, these algorithms attempt to select a trajectory that extends as far as possible to produce a smooth plan with a limited number of bandwidth changes. As a result, the trajectory for each run must eventually reach both the overflow and the underflow curves, generating a *frontier* of possible starting points for the next run (see Figure 4.1). The various bandwidth smoothing algorithms differ in how they select a starting point for run $j+1$ on rate increases and decreases, resulting in transmission plans with different performance properties:

Critical Bandwidth Allocation

Recall, the *critical bandwidth allocation* (CBA) algorithm starts a rate decrease at the leftmost point on the frontier, where the trajectory for run j hits the F_{under} curve; for rate increases, the CBA algorithm performs a search along the frontier to locate the starting point that allows the next trajectory to extend as far as possible. For any rate

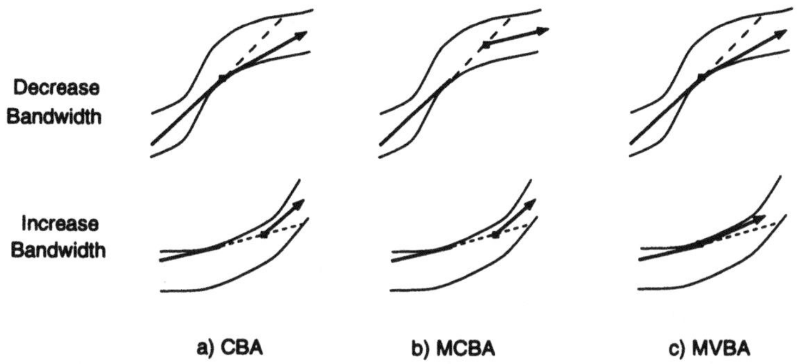

Figure 4.1: CBA, MCBA, and MVBA Plan Creation. This figure shows how the CBA, MCBA, and MVBA plans differ in their choice of starting points for each run in the bandwidth allocation plan.

change, the CBA algorithm determines the longest trajectory for run $j+1$, based on the selected starting point and initial buffer occupancy (vertical distance from F_{under}). Figure 4.1 shows an example of a bandwidth increase and decrease for the critical bandwidth allocation algorithm. Finally, this strategy results in a transmission plan that has the smallest possible peak bandwidth requirement (minimizes $max_j\{r_j\}$) and the minimum number of bandwidth *increases*.

Minimum Changes Bandwidth Allocation

To minimize the number of rate decreases, the *minimum changes bandwidth allocation* (MCBA) algorithm extends the CBA scheme to perform the linear search operation on *all* rate changes[1]. This results in a transmission plan with the smallest possible number of rate changes (minimizes m), as well as the minimum peak bandwidth requirement. The MCBA and CBA algorithms have a worst-case complexity of $O(n^2 \log n)$, where the $\log n$ term arises from performing a binary search along the frontier of each run; on average, the algorithms run in $O(n \log n)$ time. Figure 4.1 shows an example of a bandwidth increase and decrease for the MCBA algorithm.

Minimum Variability Bandwidth Allocation

Instead of minimizing m, a bandwidth smoothing algorithm can strive to reduce the *variability* in the rate requirements [SALE96]; we refer to this approach as the *minimum variability bandwidth allocation* (MVBA) algorithm. To adjust to variations in the underlying video stream, the MVBA algorithm initiates bandwidth changes at the leftmost point along the frontier of each run, for both rate increases and rate decreases. As a result, an MVBA transmission plan *gradually* alters the stream's rate requirement, sometimes at the expense of a larger number of small bandwidth

1. This bandwidth algorithm is the *optimal bandwidth allocation algorithm* presented in the last chapter.

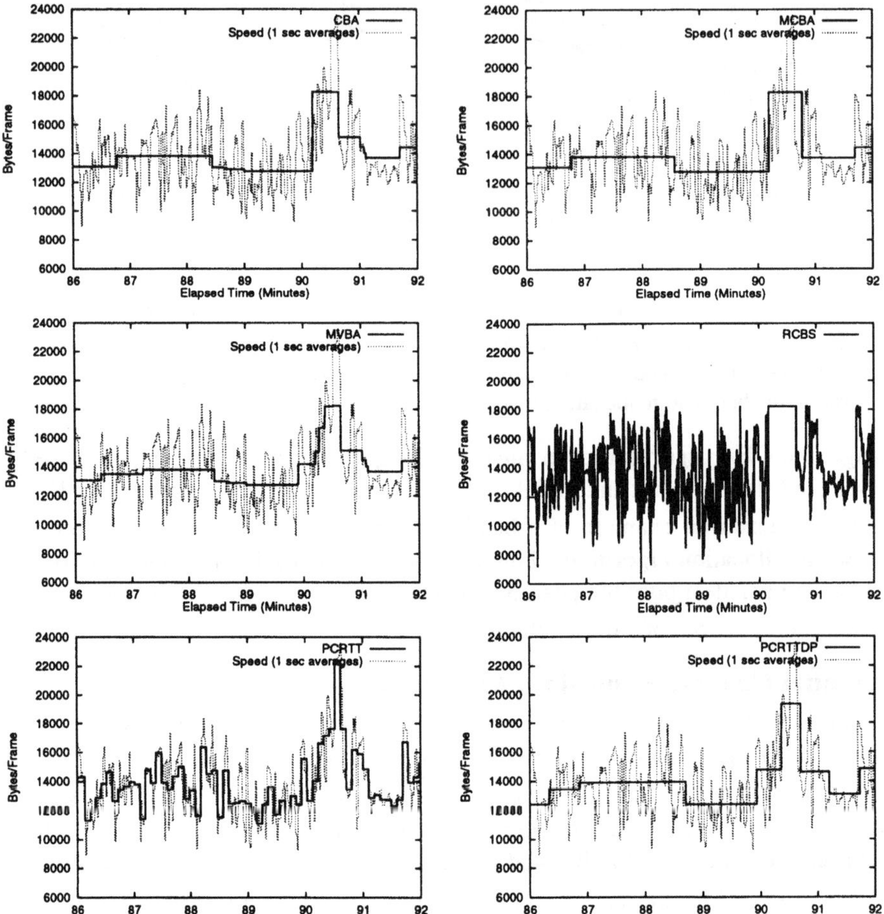

Figure 4.2: Bandwidth Plans. These graphs show the transmission plans generated by six different bandwidth smoothing algorithms, applied to the movie *Speed* and a 1 megabyte client prefetch buffer. For the PCRTT algorithm, the graph shows the plan with the largest possible interval size that would not overflow a 1 megabyte buffer.

changes. By avoiding a binary search along the frontier, the MVBA algorithm can have a worst-case complexity of $O(n^2)$; this initial algorithm can be modified to be strictly $O(n)$ [SALE96].

The MVBA and CBA algorithms handle bandwidth decreases in the same manner, while an CBA plan more closely resembles an MCBA plan on rate increases, as shown in Figure 4.2. For a given client buffer size, the CBA, MCBA, and MVBA bandwidth smoothing algorithms result in transmission plans that minimize the peak bandwidth and maximize the minimum bandwidth. Still, these algorithms differ in terms of rate variability, the frequency of rate changes, and client buffer utilization, as discussed in Section 4.3

4.2.3 Smoothing Based on F_{under}

Given the different starting points on the *frontiers*, the CBA, MCBA, and MVBA algorithms all attempt to select trajectories that extend as far as possible before reaching both the F_{under} and F_{over} curves. Other smoothing algorithms focus on the F_{under} curve in constructing a schedule; if necessary, these algorithms can iterate to compute a schedule that also satisfies the buffer constraint b for the F_{over} curve.

Rate-Constrained Bandwidth Smoothing

Given a maximum bandwidth constraint r, the *rate-constrained bandwidth smoothing* (RCBS) algorithm generates a schedule with the smallest buffer utilization by prefetching frames as late as possible [FENG97a]. In addition, given the rate r, this algorithm minimizes the maximum buffer size required for the particular rate. This O(n) algorithm starts with the last frame of the movie and sequences backwards toward the first frame. Any frame that exceeds the rate constraint is modified to the maximum rate constraint and then prefetched earlier. As shown in Figure 4.2, the RCBS plan follows the actual data rate for the movie rather closely, particularly for small buffer sizes. To minimize the peak rate requirement, as well as buffer utilization, the RCBS algorithm first invokes the O(n) MVBA algorithm to determine the smallest possible peak rate for a given buffer size; then, this rate constraint is used in computing the RCBS schedule. A more formal treatment of RCBS is provided in Section 6.3 of Chapter 6.

Piece-wise Constant Rate Transmission and Transport

In contrast to the four previous algorithms, the *piecewise constant rate transmission and transport* (PCRTT) algorithm [MCMA96] creates bandwidth allocation plans by dividing the video stream into fixed-size intervals. This O(n) algorithm generates a single run for each interval by connecting the intersection points on the F_{under} curve, as shown in Figure 4.3; the slopes of these lines correspond to the rates r_j in the resulting transmission plan. To avoid buffer underflow, the PCRTT scheme vertically offsets this plan until all of the runs lie above the F_{under} curve. Raising the plan corresponds to introducing an initial playback delay at the client site; the resulting transmission curve also determines the minimum acceptable buffer size to avoid overflow given the interval size, as shown in Figure 4.3.

PCRTT - Dynamic Programming

Instead of requiring a rate change for each time interval, a recent extension to the PCRTT algorithm employs dynamic programming (DP) to calculate a minimum-cost transmission plan that consists of m runs [MCMA97]. Although dynamic program-

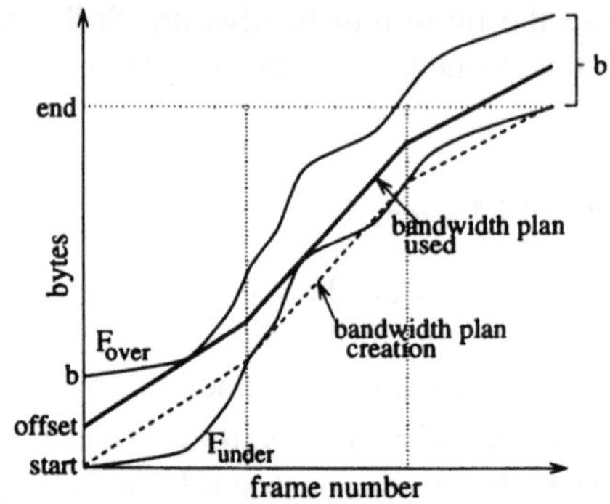

Figure 4.3: PCRTT Plan Creation. This figure shows the creation of a PCRTT bandwidth allocation plan. First, the algorithm calculates the average frame size for each interval (dashed line). Then, the algorithm raises the plan to avoid buffer underflow. Based on the offset plan, the minimum buffer requirement is the maximum distance above the underflow curve.

ming offers a general framework for optimization, we focus on the buffer size *b* as the cost metric to facilitate comparison with the other smoothing algorithms. The algorithm iteratively computes the minimum-cost schedule with *k* runs by adding a single rate changes to the best schedule with *k-1* rate changes. However, an exact solution, permitting rate changes in any time slot, would introduce significant computational complexity, particularly for full-length video traces. To reduce the computational overhead, a heuristic version of the algorithm [MCMA97] groups frames into intervals, as in Figure 4.3, when computing each candidate schedule; then, the full frame-level information is used to determine how far to raise the schedule to avoid buffer underflow. This algorithm has a computational complexity of $O(n^3)$.

As shown in Figure 4.2, the resulting PCRTT-DP algorithm, using a group size of *60* frames, produces bandwidth plans that are somewhat similar to MCBA plans, since both try to limit the number of rate changes. In contrast, the original PCRTT algorithm produces a schedule with a larger number of short runs, since the algorithm uses a single time interval throughout the video; in this example, a small interval size is necessary to avoid overflow of the client buffer. The RCBS plan changes the transmission rate in almost every time unit, except when large frames introduce smoothing at the peak rate. The next section compares the smoothing algorithms across a range of client buffer sizes, video clips, and performance metrics to evaluate these tradeoffs in transmitting prerecorded, variable-bit-rate video.

4.3 Performance Evaluation

Using the traces from the video library, this section compares the bandwidth smoothing algorithms based on a collection of performance metrics. These metrics include the peak rate requirements, the variability of the bandwidth allocations, the number of bandwidth changes, the variability of the time between bandwidth changes, and the utilization of the prefetch buffer. By applying these metrics to server transmission plans, across a wide range of realistic client buffer sizes, the simulation experiments show cost-performance trends that affect the transmission, transport, and playback of compressed video. Since some of the algorithms implicitly introduce playback delay, we permit each algorithm to prefetch data on the first bandwidth run for a fair comparison.

For the PCRTT and PCRTT-DP algorithms, which determine the buffer size as a by-product of computing the bandwidth plan, we vary the window size (for PCRTT) and the number of rate changes (for PCRTT-DP) to generate a collection of plans, each with a corresponding buffer size. The fixed window size in the PCRTT algorithm can result in fluctuations in the performance metrics as the buffer size increases, since a smaller window size can sometimes result in a larger buffer requirement. To remove these artificial fluctuations, we ensure that each data point corresponds to the PCRTT plan that has the lowest peak rate requirement for that buffer size (or smaller). The PCRTT-DP heuristic computes bandwidth plans based on groups of *60* frames to reduce computational complexity; sample experiments with smaller group sizes resulted in similar values for the performance metrics. However, the frame grouping does limit the ability of the algorithm to compute bandwidth plans for small buffer sizes; for small buffer sizes, a more exact (and computationally expensive) version of the PCRTT-DP heuristic should produce statistics that resemble the MCBA results, since both algorithms compute transmission plans than limit the number of rate changes. The frame-grouping and rate-change parameters both limit the algorithm's ability to compute valid plans for small buffer sizes, since smoothing into a small buffer requires bandwidth changes on a very small time scale.

For a typical two-hour video (*n=216,000* frames), the CBA, MCBA, MVBA, RCBS, and PCRTT algorithms require a few seconds of computation time on a modern workstation. The RCBS algorithm generally executes in the smallest amount of time (after determining the rate constraint), followed by the PCRTT, MVBA, CBA, and MCBA algorithms (in that order). The PCRTT-DP algorithm, using a group size of *60* frames and allowing up to *1000* rate changes, requires about two hours to execute. Because the PCRTT-DP algorithm start with the number of rate changes $K=1$ and iteratively calculates the minimal cost of each successive bandwidth change, calculating a plan that has *1000* bandwidth changes requires the calculation of all plans with fewer bandwidth changes. To speed this algorithm up, we calculated all the costs (in terms of the buffer size) for each sequence of frames (i, j), $0 < i < j \leq N$. This reduces the computational complexity of each bandwidth change to $O(n^2)$.

4.3.1 Peak Bandwidth Requirement

The peak rate of a smoothed video stream determines the worst-case bandwidth requirement across the path from the video storage on the server, the route through the

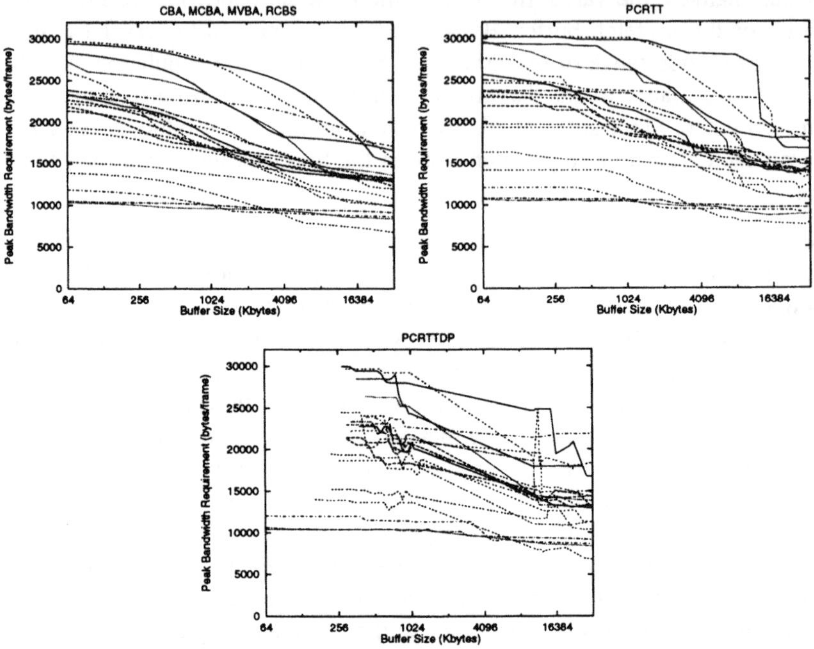

Figure 4.4: Peak Bandwidth Requirement. These graphs plot the peak rate requirements for the various smoothing algorithms as a function of the client buffer size. The CBA, MCBA, MVBA, and RCBS algorithms generate transmission plans with the same peak rate.

network, and the prefetch buffer at the client site. Hence, most bandwidth smoothing algorithms attempt to minimize

$$max_j \{r_j\}$$

to increase the likelihood that the server, network, and the client have sufficient resources to handle the stream. This is especially important if the service must reserve network bandwidth based on the peak rate, or if the client has a low-bandwidth connection to the network. In addition, reducing the maximum bandwidth requirement permits the server to multiplex a larger number of streams. Figure 4.4 plots $max\{r_j\}$ for each of the six smoothing algorithms, as a function of the client buffer size. The CBA, MCBA, MVBA, and RCBS algorithms all result in the minimum peak bandwidth requirement given a fixed buffer size, as discussed in Section 4.2.

The CBA, MCBA, MVBA, and RCBS algorithms have monotonically decreasing peak bandwidth requirements as the buffer size grows. Under medium-sized buffers, these algorithms produces smaller peak rates than the two PCRTT algorithms by prefetching data as far in advance as the buffer allows. In contrast, the PCRTT is limited by the interval size. Still, for most buffer sizes, the PCRTT plans do not have significantly larger peak requirements, suggesting that the algorithm makes fairly good

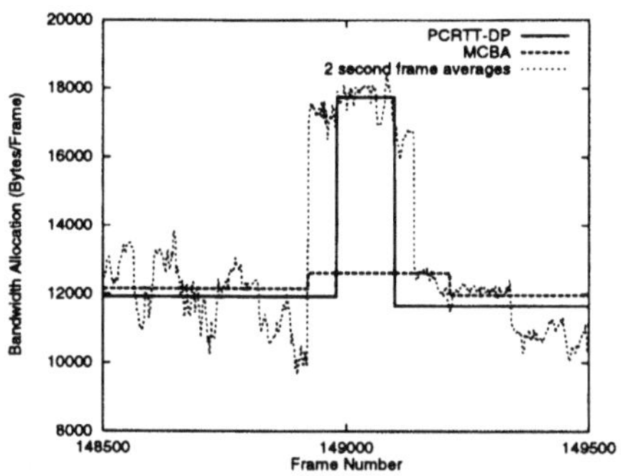

Figure 4.5: PCRTT-DP Frame Grouping. This graph plots the PCRTT-DP and MCBA plans for the movie *Speed* with a *1*-megabyte prefetch buffer. Using a group size of *60* frames, the PCRTT-DP plan has a larger peak-rate run because the region of large frames extends part way into adjoining groups. In contrast, the MCBA algorithm can reduce the peak rate by transmitting more of the large frames during a portion of the previous time interval.

use of the smoothing buffer. The PCRTT algorithm has the most difficulty with video clips that have areas of sustained large frames followed by areas of small frames (or vice-versa), which require small interval sizes to avoid buffer overflow and underflow; these small intervals limit the algorithm's ability to employ prefetching to smooth the large frames in the underlying compressed video stream.

The PCRTT-DP plans have smaller peak bandwidth requirements than the PCRTT algorithm and similar to the other algorithms. In fact, an exact version of PCRTT-DP algorithm, using a group size of *1* frame, would generate transmission plans that minimize the peak bandwidth. However, the grouping of frames can sometimes inflate the peak rate when a sequence of large frames fall within a single group, as shown in Figure 4.5. In this particular example, smoothing the peak over the previous group of *60* frames would result in a smaller peak bandwidth requirement at the expense of a larger buffer size. The MCBA algorithm is able to adjust the bandwidth requirement at any frame, allowing it to suitably adjust the start and end of the run at frame 149,000. Referring to Figure 4.5, note that this high-bandwidth run starts and ends less than one group of frames away from the corresponding run in the PCRTT-DP plan. Still, in most cases, the PCRTT-DP heuristic can produce plans with nearly optimal peak bandwidth requirements.

Under small buffer sizes, the movies with the largest variations in frame sizes also tend to have the largest peak bandwidth requirements, due to the limited ability to smooth large peaks. In all of the plots, the *Beauty and the Beast*, *E.T. (quality 100)*, and *NCAA Final Four* videos are the top three curves, while the *Seminar* videos have the lowest peak bandwidth requirements for buffer sizes less than *1* megabyte. For the three *E.T.* videos, the lower-quality encodings have lower peak rate requirements, due to the smaller frame sizes at each point in the video. In fact, under larger buffer sizes,

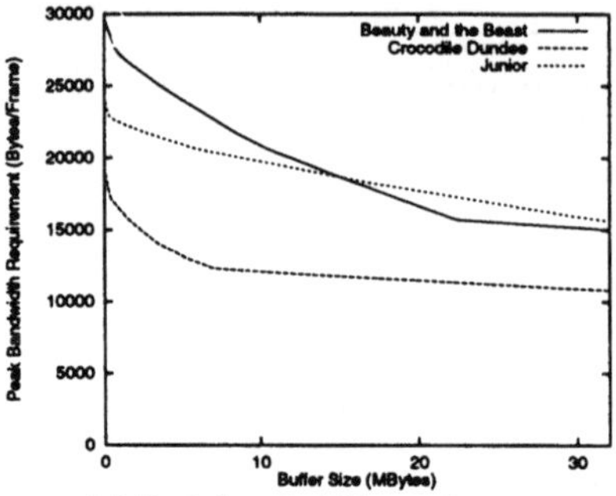

(a) Peak bandwidth vs. *b*

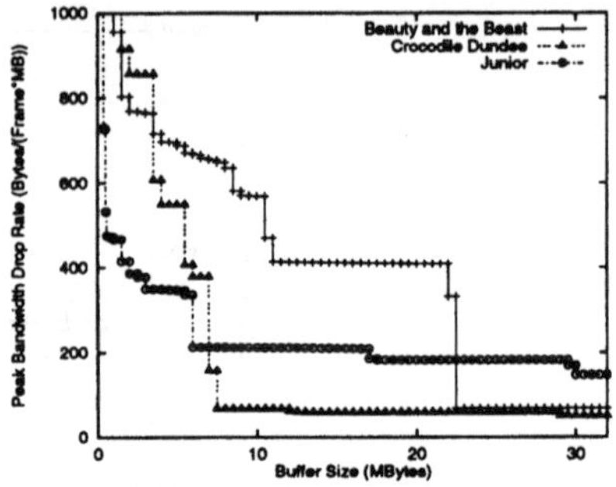

(b) Peak rate derivative

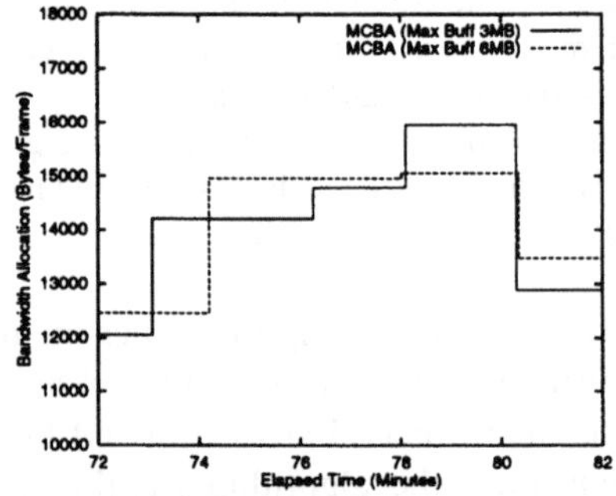

(c) Buffering Example

Figure 4.6: Reducing the Peak Rate. These plots highlight the relationship between the peak bandwidth metric and the client buffer size. In (a), we has selected 3 representative movies *Beauty and the Beast*, *Crocodile Dundee*, and *Junior*. In (b), the derivative (slope between peak bandwidth, buffer points) are shown, emphasizing the linear reduction in peak bandwidth requirement.

the *E.T. (quality 75)* video actually has a *lower* peak bandwidth than the *Seminar* videos. For large client buffers, prefetching removes nearly all of the burstiness in the stream, yielding a plan that stays very close to the mean frame size of *6305* bytes; the three *Seminar* videos, digitized with a quality factor of *90*, have larger average frame sizes (*8604*, *8835*, and *9426* bytes). Thus, for small buffer sizes, the peak bandwidth requirement is generally driven by the *maximum* frame size, while for larger buffer sizes, the peak rate is driven mostly by the *average* frame size.

Although a large prefetch buffer can substantially reduce the peak rate, the addition of more buffer space offers diminishing returns beyond a certain point. Figure 4.6(a) further illustrates this effect by plotting the peak-bandwidth curves for *Beauty and the Beast*, *Crocodile Dundee*, and *Junior* with a linear scale on the x-axis. Each curve consists of a sequence of linear segments that become less steep as the buffer size increases, as shown in Figure 4.6(b) which plots the magnitude of the slopes. Typically, the peak bandwidth in a transmission plan is determined by a region of large frames in a small portion of the movie. As the buffer size grows, the peak-rate run becomes shorter and wider due to more aggressive prefetching, as shown in Figure 4.6(c). Eventually, the buffer size grows large enough for this run to reach a region of small frames that can allow a more dramatic reduction in the bandwidth requirement; at this point, the peak rate may occur in a different part of video, also resulting in a new linear segment in the peak-bandwidth curve. Based on this observation, the server could characterize the buffer-bandwidth trade-off as a small number of linear curves, allowing efficient admission control policies that balance the use of network/server bandwidth and client buffer space.

4.3.2 Variability in Bandwidth Requirements

In addition to minimizing the peak bandwidth, a smoothing algorithm should reduce the overall *variability* in the rate requirements for the video stream[SALE96]. Intuitively, plans with smaller rate variation should require fewer resources from the server and the network; more precisely, smoother plans have lower effective bandwidth requirements, allowing the server and the network to statistically multiplex a larger number of streams. Even under a deterministic model of resource reservation, the server's ability to change a stream's bandwidth reservation may depend on the *size* of the adjustment ($|r_{j+1} - r_j|$), particularly on rate *increases*. If the system does not support advance booking of resources, the server or the network may be unable to acquire enough bandwidth to start transmitting frames at the higher rate[1]. Since the video clips have different average rate requirements, varying from *1.51* to *3.95* megabits/second, Figure 4.7 plots the *coefficient of variation*

$$\frac{stdev\{c_0, c_1, \ldots, c_{n-1}\}}{\frac{1}{n}\sum_{i=0}^{n-1} c_i}$$

to normalize the variability metric across the different streams.

In Figure 4.7, the MVBA plans have the smallest variability in bandwidth allocations, since the algorithm optimizes this metric. Since the CBA algorithm is the same as the MVBA algorithm for bandwidth decreases, it has nearly the same variability across the various videos. For small buffer sizes, the MCBA algorithm has nearly the same variability in bandwidth requests as the other algorithms since they have to perform rate changes on a small time scale; for larger buffer sizes, the MCBA algorithm has more latitude in combining bandwidth requests, resulting in greater rate variability than MVBA and CBA. For the videos in Figure 4.7, the MCBA plans have rate variations that are approximately *5%* larger than the corresponding MVBA plans. In vid-

---

1. If the system cannot reserve resources for the higher bandwidth r_{j+1}, the video stream may have to adapt to a smaller rate to avoid terminating the remainder of the transfer. For example, with a *layered* encoding of the video stream, the server could reduce the transmission rate by sending only the higher priority components of the stream. To limit the degradation in video quality at the client site, the server can raise the stream's rate as close to r_{j+1} as possible.

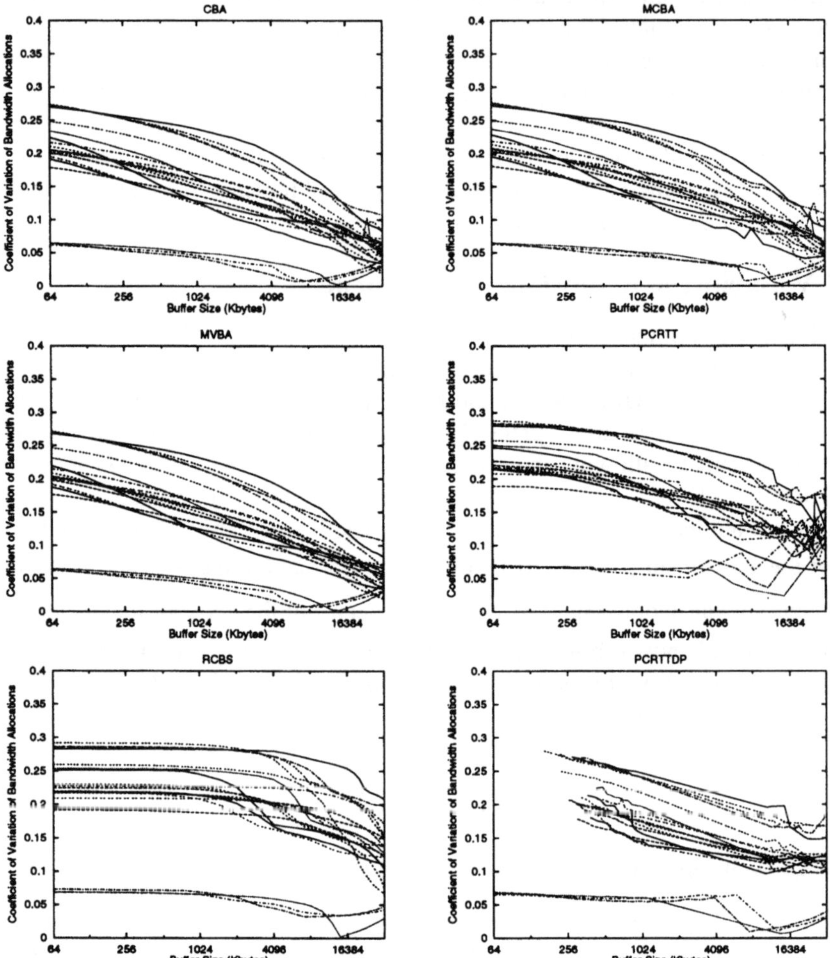

Figure 4.7: Bandwidth Variability. This figure shows the normalized standard deviation of bandwidth allocations (on a per frame basis) for the various smoothing algorithms, as a function of the client buffer size.

eos where the MCBA algorithm has much fewer bandwidth changes than the MVBA, the MCBA algorithm results in higher variability of bandwidth requests. Still, the MVBA, CBA, and MCBA plans have similar variability metrics, while also minimizing the peak rate and maximizing the minimum rate [FENG95, FENG96, SALE96, FENG97a], so all three algorithms should produce transmission plans with low effective bandwidth requirements.

In contrast, the RCBS plans have greater rate variability, particularly under larger buffer sizes, since the algorithm limits prefetching unless it is necessary to avoid

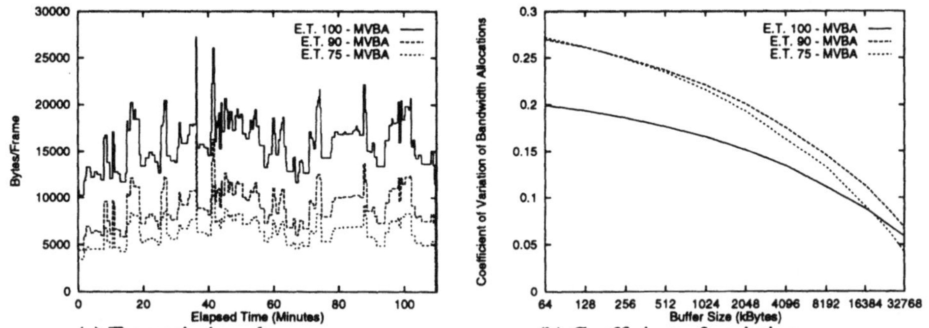

(a) Transmission plans (b) Coefficient of variation

Figure 4.8: Rate Variability of *E.T.* Encodings. These graphs evaluate the three traces of *E.T.* (with quality levels of *100*, *90*, and *75*), using the MVBA algorithm and a *1* megabyte buffer. Despite reducing the bandwidth requirements, the coarser encodings exhibit greater rate variability, relative to the average frame size.

increasing the peak rate. As a result, an RCBS plan often transmits small frames at a low rate, resulting in a much lower minimum bandwidth than the MVBA, CBA, and MCBA algorithms. Hence, the modest increase in rate variability under the RCBS algorithm stems from the *small* frames, instead of the large frames as one would expect from an unsmoothed transfer of the video. The PCRTT algorithm has the largest variability in bandwidth allocations. Because the PCRTT algorithm smooths bandwidth requests based on fixed interval lengths, it cannot smooth burst of large frames beyond the size of the interval, resulting in higher peaks and lower valleys. As buffer sizes get larger, the partitioning of the frames into fixed intervals plays a large role in determining the minimum amount of buffering required to have continuous playback of the video.

For all the algorithms, the Beauty and the Beast, *E.T. (quality 75)*, and *E.T. (quality 90)* videos exhibit the most bandwidth variability. Interestingly, the *E.T.* streams with *lower* quality factors have greater variability in the bandwidth requirements, as shown in Figure 4.8. Although a coarser encoding reduces the *average* frame size, some frame lengths decrease more than others, depending on the scale of detail in the scene; from the information in Table 2.3, the coefficient of variation for frame sizes is *0.29*, *0.28*, and *0.20* for quality factors of *75*, *90*, and *100*, respectively. Under small buffer sizes, the larger variability in frame sizes translates into larger variability in the bandwidth requirements. For larger buffer sizes, the three versions of *E.T.* have similar bandwidth variability, due to the common long-term variation in scene content; the variability of the *E.T. (quality 75)* clip decreases more quickly, as a function of buffer size, since a larger prefetch buffer can absorb most of the variation in frame sizes for the lower quality stream.

4.3.3 Number of Bandwidth Changes

To reduce the complexity of the server and client sites, a bandwidth smoothing algorithm could strive to minimize *m*, the number of runs in the transmission schedule. A rate change alters the amount of data that the server must read from the disk in each time interval, which can have implications for disk layout and scheduling policies, particularly when the server must multiplex a large number of video streams. Also, smaller values of *m* reduce the storage requirements for the bandwidth plans, although this is typically small in comparison to the size of the actual video data. Minimizing the number of rate changes can also limit the cost of negotiating with the network [GROS95] to reserve link bandwidth for transporting the video stream[1].

Figure 4.9 compares the algorithms based on the number of bandwidth changes in the server transmission plan for each of the clips in the video library. Since the video clips have different lengths, varying from *41* minutes to *122* minutes, the graphs plot the *frequency* of bandwidth changes

$$\frac{m}{\sum_{j=0}^{m-1} t_j}$$

in changes per minute across a range of client buffer sizes.

For all of the smoothing algorithms and video traces, the client prefetch buffer is effective in reducing the frequency of rate change operations. In each graph, the bottom three curves correspond to the *Seminar* videos, which do not require many rate changes due to their small frame sizes and the low variability in their bandwidth requirements. The *NCAA Final Four* video requires the highest rate of bandwidth changes, due to the large frame sizes and long-term variations in scene content; for a *64* kilobyte buffer, this stream requires an average of *1.8*, *4.9*, and *8.5* rate changes per minute under the MCBA, CBA, and MVBA plans, respectively. In general, the CBA and MVBA plans result in approximately *3* and *6* times as many changes as MCBA algorithm, which minimizes *m*. For some movies and buffer sizes, the MVBA plans have up to *14* times as many bandwidth changes as the corresponding MCBA plans. This occurs because the MVBA algorithm introduces a larger number of small rate changes to minimize the variability of bandwidth requirements in the server transmission plan.

As an extreme example, we compare the MCBA and MVBA algorithms on the *23*-second video trace shown in Figure 4.10(a). For a *128* kilobyte buffer, the MVBA algorithm introduces *104* rate changes (55 increases and 49 decreases), while the MCBA plan has just three bandwidth changes, as shown in Figure 4.10(b). During the

1. To further reduce interaction with the network, each video stream could have a separate *reservation plan* for allocating network resources along the route to the client. This reservation plan could have fewer rate changes than the underlying transmission plan, at the expense of reserving excess link bandwidth [GROS95, SALE96]

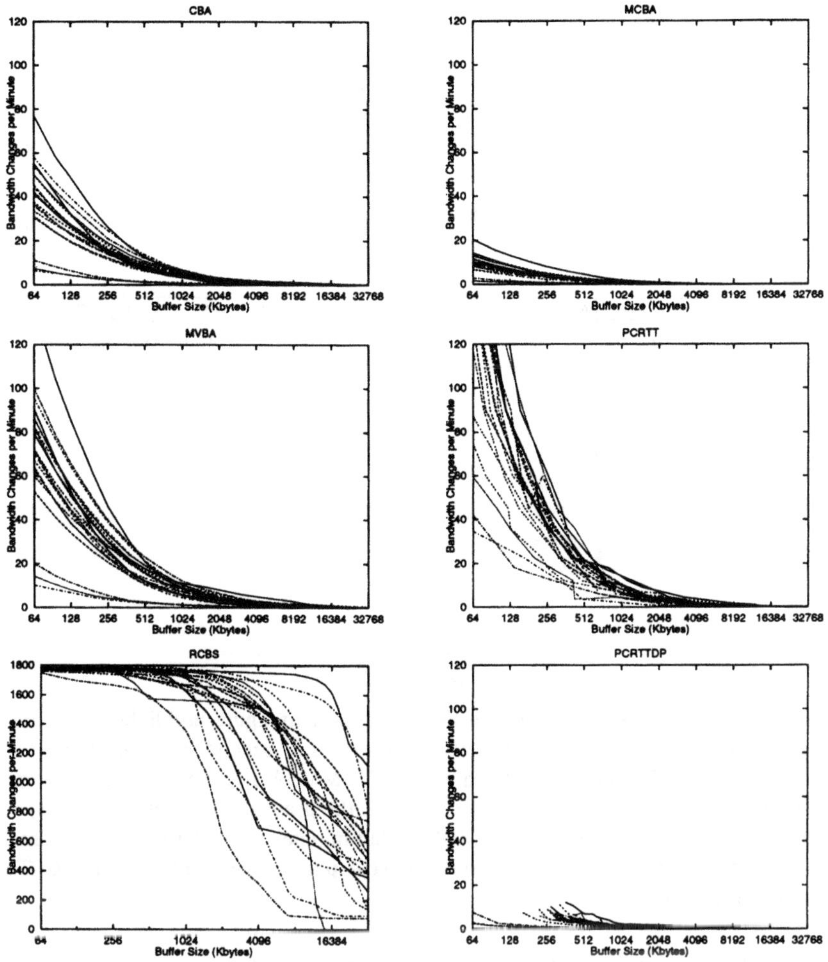

Figure 4.9: Rate of Bandwidth Changes. These graphs show the rate of bandwidth changes required for the various smoothing algorithms as a function of the client buffer size. Note that the RCBS graph has a *much* wider range of values on the y-axis, compared to the plots for the other five algorithms.

first *400* frames of the video segment, the frame sizes gradually increase over time. On this long stretch of increasing bandwidth requirements, the MVBA algorithm tends to follow the "curve" of the increase by generating a sequence of small rate increases. A similar effect occurs during the gradual decreases in frame sizes for the remainder video segment. In Figure 4.10(b), note that the area between the two plans, in the range of frames *12720* to *12900*, is approximately equal to the size of the smoothing buffer. This suggests that the MVBA plan has filled the client buffer, requiring a more gradual response to the rate increases in the video segment. In con-

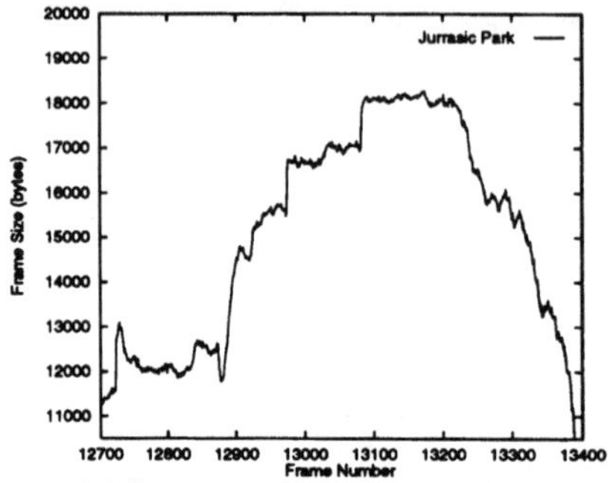

(a) Segment of *Jurassic Park*

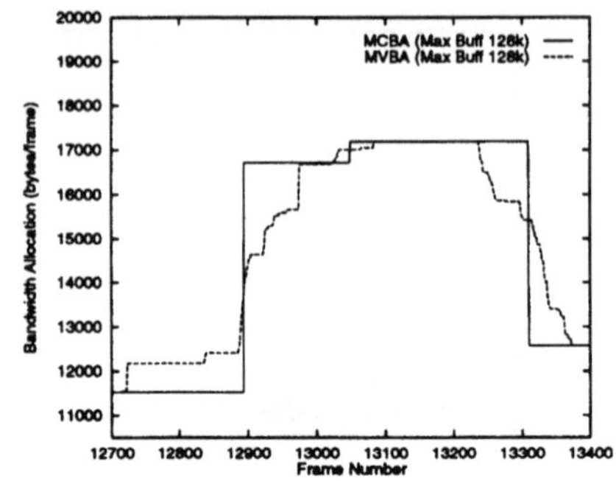

(b) MCBA and MVBA plans

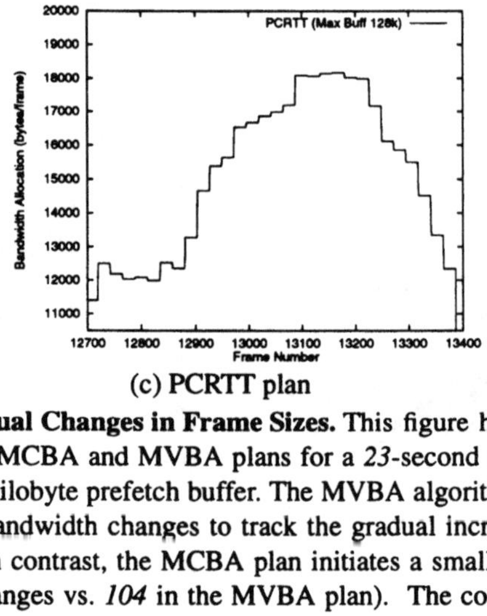

(c) PCRTT plan

Figure 4.10: Gradual Changes in Frame Sizes. This figure highlights the differences between the MCBA and MVBA plans for a *23*-second segment of *Jurassic Park* under a *128*-kilobyte prefetch buffer. The MVBA algorithm performs a large number of small bandwidth changes to track the gradual increases (decreases) in the frame sizes. In contrast, the MCBA plan initiates a smaller number of larger rate changes (*3* changes vs. *104* in the MVBA plan). The corresponding PCRTT plan has *31* rate changes.

trast, the MCBA plan has a nearly empty buffer, giving the algorithm greater latitude in adjusting the server transmission rate; referring to Figure 4.10(b), this is a case where the MCBA algorithm selects a starting point at the *rightmost* point along the frontier whereas the MVBA algorithm selects the *leftmost* point.

Although the MVBA plans typically have fewer rate changes than the corresponding PCRTT plans, the PCRTT algorithm sometimes generates fewer rate changes under moderate buffer sizes. For these buffer sizes, the PCRTT algorithm is effective at combining several bandwidth runs of the MVBA algorithm into a single rate interval. For example, in Figure 4.10(c), the PCRTT algorithm generates only *31* rate changes, in contrast to the *104* changes in the corresponding MVBA plan. The PCRTT-DP algorithm produces bandwidth allocation plans that are very similar to the MCBA algorithm, since they both strive to minimize the number of rate changes; however, under smaller buffer sizes, the PCRTT-DP heuristic generate more bandwidth changes due to the frame-grouping factor. In contrast to the PCRTT algorithms, the RCBS plans tend to follow the sizes of the individual frames for most of the stream, except when some prefetching is necessary to avoid increasing the peak rate for transmitting the video. With a small client buffer, the RCBS algorithm requires nearly *1800* rate changes per minute, as shown in Figure 4.9; in the absence of any smoothing, a *30* frames/second rate would correspond to at most *2400* changes per minute. Although the number of rate changes decreases as the buffer size grows, the RCBS algorithm still generates significantly more bandwidth changes than the other algorithms except for extremely large buffer sizes.

4.3.4 Periodicity of Bandwidth Requests

In addition to minimizing the frequency of bandwidth changes, the server may also wish to limit the total number of rate changes that can occur during an interval of time. In between rate changes, the server can transmit the smoothed video without altering the underlying transmission schedule. Hence, a bandwidth smoothing algorithm may try to enforce a lower bound on the minimum time between rate changes to reduce the overhead in multiplexing a large number of video streams. In addition, in networks that support advance booking of resources, periodic bandwidth allocation intervals can reduce the complexity of the admission control algorithms by ensuring that reservations change only at a relatively small set of points [FERR95]. While Section 4.3.3 evaluates the *average* rate of bandwidth changes, the plots in Figure 4.11 focus on the *variability* of this metric. Since the bandwidth plans have different average run lengths, the graphs plot

$$\frac{stdev\{t_0, t_1, \ldots, t_{m-1}\}}{\frac{1}{m}\Sigma_{i=0}^{m-1} t_i}$$

to compare the "periodicity" of bandwidth requests. Smaller values imply that the transmission plan has run lengths that stay close to the mean values.

Ideally, in fact, the transmission plans should impose a lower bound on the minimum time between rate changes ($min_j\{t_j\}$). However, only the PCRTT algorithms produce meaningful values for $min_j\{t_j\}$, since the plans are constructed from fixed-size intervals; in fact, the coefficient of variation is *0* for the PCRTT algorithm. The MCBA, CBA, MVBA, and RCBS algorithms typically have one or more runs with extremely short durations; for most buffer sizes less than *2* megabytes, $min_j\{t_j\}$ is just one or two frame slots. For the most part, the MCBA algorithm results in less variability than the CBA and MVBA algorithms, which can introduce a large number of small bandwidth changes, even under fairly large buffer sizes. The RCBS plans have *much* larger variability, since the transmission plans consists of a mixture of large run lengths (where frames have been smoothed at the peak rate) and small run lengths (where no prefetching occurs). To reduce the frequency of rate changes, generalizations of the RCBS algorithm could transmit frames at averaged rates over small intervals of time

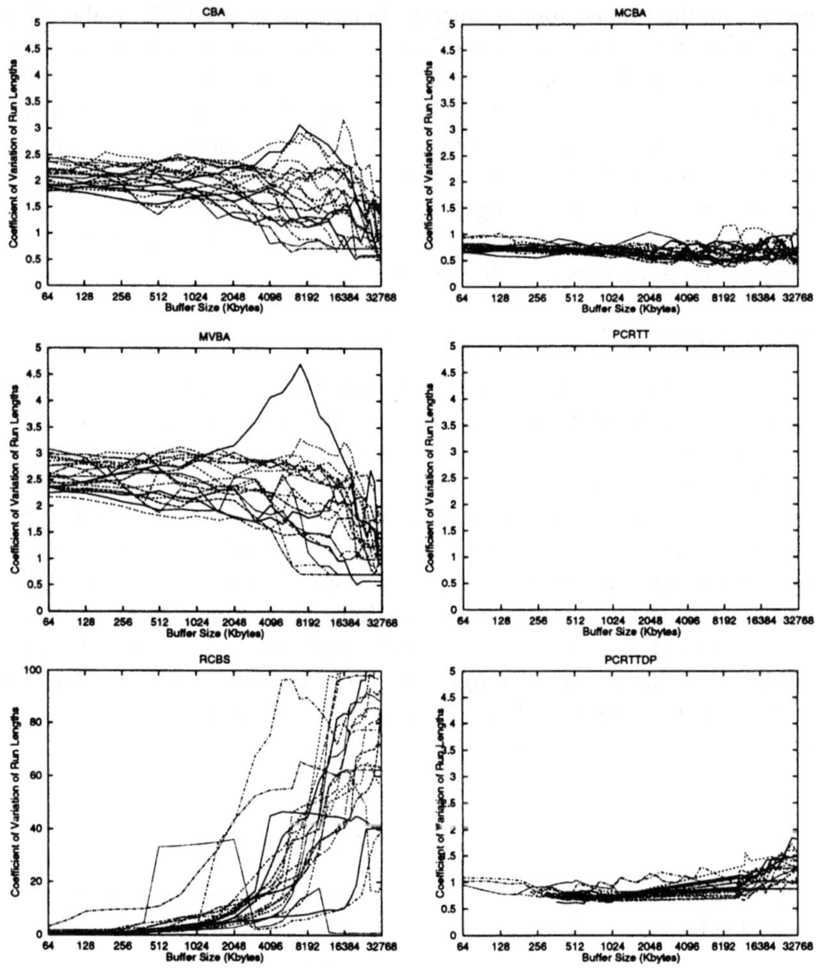

Figure 4.11: Bandwidth Length Variability. This figure shows the coefficient of variation for the bandwidth run lengths as a function of the client buffer size. Note that the RCBS plot has a different y-axis scale than the other graphs.

by introducing a modest amount of extra prefetching[FENG97a]. This hybrid of the PCRTT and RCBS algorithms would produce plans with a reasonable time between consecutive rate changes, while still limiting the amount of prefetching.

Under small buffer sizes, the top three curves for the MCBA algorithm correspond to the *Seminar* videos. These videos have a small number of short frames, followed by a large number of long frames; under a small prefetch buffer, the server cannot continually transmit frames at a high rate when the client is consuming the short frames. As a result, the bandwidth plan consists of a mixture of short and long run lengths, causing greater variability than the other videos; under a larger buffer size, the plans become much more "periodic." As shown in the MVBA graph in Figure 4.11, one movie (*Beauty and the Beast*) exhibits a particularly high variation of run-lengths. Compared to the other videos, this movie has longer sustained regions of large and small frames. Using a larger buffer smooths the *tops* and *bottoms* of the bandwidth plans, combining relatively larger areas into even larger areas while still leaving many smaller rate adjustments in the transitions. As the number of changes starts to decrease with large buffer sizes, the plans generated by the MVBA algorithm approach the plans that are generated by the MCBA algorithm.

4.3.5 Buffer Utilization

Although bandwidth smoothing reduces the rate requirements for transmitting stored video, prefetching may consume significant buffer resources at the client site. For a given size b for the playback buffer, a smoothing algorithm could strive to limit buffer utilization while still minimizing the peak rate. Reducing the amount of prefetching allows the client to statistically share the playback space between multiple video streams, or even other applications. If the client application can perform VCR functions, such as rewinding or indexing to arbitrary points in the video stream, a bandwidth plan that limits prefetching also avoids wasting server and network resources on transmitting frames ahead of the playback point. With fewer future frames in the prefetch buffer, the client can cache multiple frames behind the current playback point, allowing the service to satisfy small VCR rewind requests directly at the client site. Figure 4.12 plots the average buffer utilization as a function of buffer size b for each of the smoothing algorithms.

Buffer utilization corresponds to how far the transmission plan lies above the F_{under} curve, on average. The MCBA and MVBA plans have buffer utilizations of approximately *50%* across most of the video traces, since these two algorithms do not differentiate between rate increases and rate decreases when computing bandwidth runs. Hence, the runs have a nearly even split between trajectories that hit F_{under} and trajectories that hit F_{over}; runs between the two constraint curves experience a progression in buffer utilization from 0%% to 100%, or vice versa, as shown in Figure 4.13(a). In contrast, the CBA algorithm tends to stay closer to the F_{under} curve by behaving like MCBA on bandwidth increases and MVBA on bandwidth decreases, as shown in Figure 4.1. As a result, the CBA plans have lower buffer utilization than the corresponding MCBA and MVBA plans. Although these three algorithms typically have *40--50%* buffer utilization, the *Seminar1* video has higher utilization under large buffer sizes, as shown by the lone higher curve in CBA, MCBA, and MVBA plots in Figure 4.12. The larger buffer sizes permit the algorithms to smooth the *Seminar1* video with a single bandwidth run, so the transmission plan never oscillates back and forth between the F_{under} and F_{over} curves.

The PCRTT plans typically have the highest buffer utilization. Drawing on the exam-

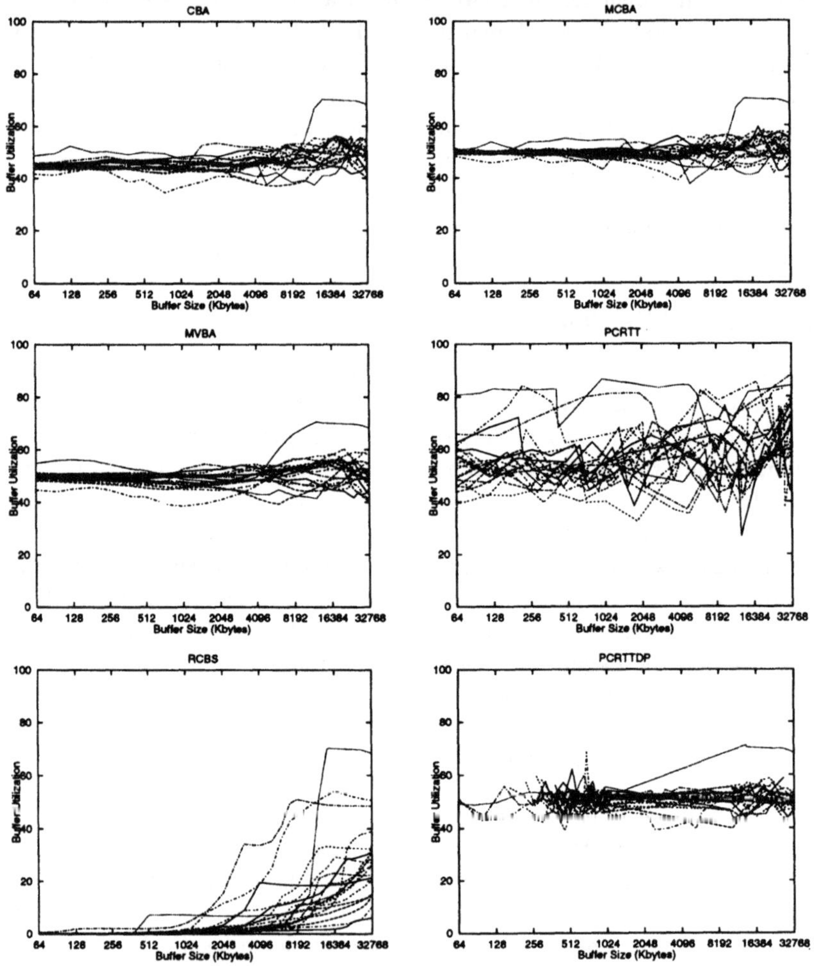

Figure 4.12: Buffer Utilization. This figure shows the average utilization of the client prefetch buffer for the various smoothing algorithms, as a function of the client buffer size.

ple in Figure 4.3, the PCRTT algorithm generates trajectories based on F_{under} and then raises the plan until no points remain below F_{under}, as shown in Figure 4.3. As a result, the final plan has very few points that lie close to F_{under}, as shown by the example in Figure 4.13(b). In contrast, RCBS plans stay as close to the F_{under} curve as possible, without increasing the peak rate requirement. In fact, an RCBS plan only reaches the F_{over} curve during the bandwidth runs that must transmit frames at the peak rate; for example, the RCBS plan has less than 15% buffer utilization for most of the video clip in Figure 4.13(c). The RCBS algorithm generates transmission plans

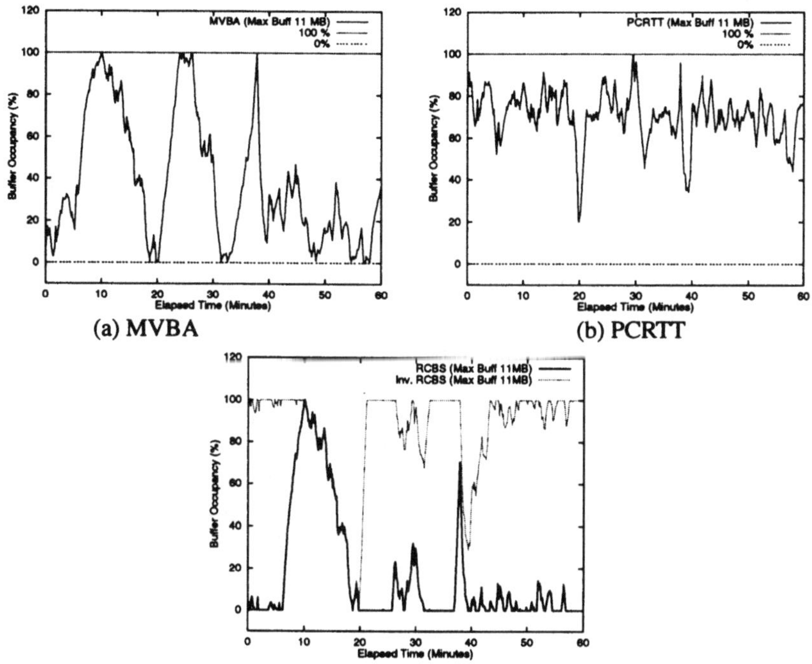

(a) MVBA (b) PCRTT

(c) Inverse RCBS

Figure 4.13: Buffer Utilization. This figure shows the buffer utilization over time for smoothing the movie *Crocodile Dundee* with an *11*-megabyte prefetch buffer.

with much lower buffer usage than the other algorithms, especially under small buffer sizes. Buffer utilization is especially low for small values of b, where very few frames are prefetched; for larger b values, even RCBS performs must perform more extensive prefetching to successfully minimize the peak rate. Still, the RCBS algorithm gives the client sites the greatest latitude in sharing the prefetch buffer amongst multiple streams or in supporting efficient rewind operations.

Although low buffer utilization permits greater resource sharing and efficient VCR operations, some video-on-demand services may benefit from more aggressive prefetching, depending on the characteristics of the network connection between the server and client sites. If packets experience variable delay or significant loss rates, the service may perform more aggressive prefetching to mask the network latency (or retransmission delay). To *maximize* buffer utilization, the server could employ an algorithm that is conceptually similar to RCBS. However, instead of transmitting frames as late as possible, under the constraint on peak bandwidth, this algorithm would transmit frames as *early* as possible to tolerate larger network latency. Hence, the server would transmit frames at the peak rate, except when the transmission rate must be reduced to avoid buffer overflow at the client site. Figure 4.13(c) compares this new algorithm to the corresponding RCBS plan to highlight the upper and lower limits on buffer utilization; all other bandwidth plans that minimize the peak-rate requirement have buffer utilizations between these two curves.

4.4 Summary

In this chapter, we have presented a comprehensive comparison of bandwidth smoothing algorithms for compressed, prerecorded video. By capitalizing on the *a priori* knowledge of frame lengths, these algorithms can significantly reduce the burstiness of resource requirements for the transmission, transfer, and playback of prerecorded video. For small buffer sizes, the PCRTT algorithm is useful in creating plans that have near optimal peak bandwidth requirements while requiring very little computation time to calculate. For larger buffer sizes, however, the PCRTT algorithm limits the ability of the server to prefetch frames across interval boundaries. The CBA, MCBA, and MVBA algorithms exhibit similar performance for the peak rate requirement and the variability of bandwidth allocations; the MCBA algorithm, however, is much more effective at reducing the total number of rate changes. The RCBS algorithm introduces a large number of rate changes, and a wide variability in the bandwidth requirements, to minimize the utilization of the client prefetch buffer.

5

INTERACTIVITY IN VIDEO-ON-DEMAND SYSTEMS

5.1 Introduction

The delivery of constant quality compressed video requires that the network adapt to large fluctuations in bandwidth. We have shown that bandwidth smoothing techniques are effective in removing burstiness, making network resource scheduling simpler. In this chapter, we describe how critical bandwidth based smoothing techniques affect the underlying services in an interactive video-on-demand service. As previously mentioned, the benefits of smoothing for live video applications are constrained by the requirement that latency remain low between video capture and video playback. Stored video applications, on the other hand, can schedule the network bandwidth resources well in advance of the playback of the video. The use of in-advance reservations in such bandwidth smoothing schemes, however, has implications on the ability to provide users with familiar video cassette recorder (VCR) functionality such as stop, pause, rewind, and fast forward.

For constant quality video delivery, the video bandwidth requirements can be smoothed by prefetching data into a buffer, shifting bursts of large frames forward in time. Depending on the amount of buffering available, a frame may sit in the client's smoothing buffer for a shorter or longer time before it is played back. Long buffer residency times are often required to reduce large peak bandwidth requirements. Despite these long buffer residency times, the rate of transmission and the rate of consumption remain coupled. Alterations in the consumption rate that occur with VCR functions will require alteration in the video delivery plan, lest the buffer overflow or underflow. In addition to the goal of high network utilization, a video-on-demand system must effectively handle the contradictory goals of smoothing and responsiveness.

For video-on-demand systems with little or no buffering, the clients and servers must be tightly coupled. Any change in consumption of video data from the client must be immediately and continuously handled by the server. With buffering, changes in consumption still require an adjustment by the server. These adjustments, however, need not be made instantaneously. Many operations can be performed without requiring the delivery of any new data from the server. Larger buffers allow greater latitude in handling these stops, starts, and rewinds. With excess buffering specifically used for handling variations in consumption rate, it is possible to further decrease the required disruptions of the server by combining the changes in consumption into a few requests. The number of disruptions that the servers must handle is proportional to the buffer size used. If a majority of the rate changes can be handled by the client machine, then the network and servers can devote their resources to handling the special cases that may arise instead of handling cases which can be taken care of with appropriate buffering.

In this chapter, we discuss a framework for providing VCR functionality and in-advance bandwidth reservations within a bandwidth-smoothing, stored-video environment. We introduce the notion of *VCR-window*, the set of buffered frames within which full-function VCR capabilities are available without requiring changes to the bandwidth reservations. The size of the VCR-window is determined by the size of the client buffer. We expect that for reasonable buffer sizes a large proportion of VCR operations can be handled from the VCR-window, with the remainder requiring more involved client and server interactions. For accesses outside the VCR-window, we describe a strategy for using a *contingency channel* for users to renegotiate temporary bandwidth so that their plans can return to the bandwidth originally reserved. The use of the VCR-window along with the contingency channel affects the way in-advance reservations can be handled. We discuss the impact of providing VCR functionality on *a priori* bandwidth reservations and present a reservation system for interactive video-on-demand systems. Our results show that the VCR-window can be implemented with a small amount of additional buffering with little modifications necessary to the bandwidth reservations.

In Section 5.3, we describe the problems associated with providing VCR function capabilities to users and introduce a solution for providing limited VCR function capabilities. In Section 5.4, we present an admission control algorithm for video-on-demand resources. Using this framework, we then describe a resource reservation mechanism for critical bandwidth allocation based video delivery systems. Finally, in Section 5.5, we present the experimental simulations used to evaluate VCR-functionality in bandwidth smoothing environments.

5.2 Motivation

5.2.1 Video Playback Applications

Interactive video-on-demand encompasses a large range of applications. Because the social and economic impacts of video-on-demand systems are not yet understood, we

Application	Description
Movies-on-demand	Customers can select and play movies
Video-on-demand	Customers can access archived television and sporting events.
Interactive News T.V	An interactive newscast where customers selectively define which stories are played back.
Catalog Browsing	Customers view commercials for goods and services.
Distance Learning	Customers can view lectures on selected topics of their choice.

Table 5.1: Video Interactivity. This table lists some common applications of video on demand services that may be used in the future.

can only offer a list of expected applications. As an example, consider broadcast television programming that is in use today. Television stations solicit companies to pay for commercial slots to generate revenue. If television becomes true video-on-demand, however, only a few commercials would ever be viewed in their entirety, thus undermining their purpose. In such a situation, we can probably expect video-on-demand suppliers to provide "catalog" type services for users who wish to browse commercial offerings. Several services that have been talked about in the literature are shown in Table 5.1. The actual requirements for interactivity and the load placed on the underlying network depends heavily on the type of application. Because interactive news consists of many smaller pieces of video, the video server can expect more variation in access patterns, especially for news items that the customer does not find interesting. Movies, on the other hand, are longer running and are focused on a single theme. As a result, the amount of interaction may not be as large.

For bandwidth smoothing environments, the size, length, and burstiness of the video affects the way that VCR functions can be provided. In a server that typically handles small clips, all the videos may be downloaded to the client and all interactions are then serviced from the buffer. For servers that handle medium length clips (on the order of 15 to 45 minute length clips), the application of the CBA algorithm results in a single monotonically decreasing sequence of bandwidths for all clips with small amounts of buffering. In this case, the server can take advantage of the monotonically decreasing sequences to schedule the network effectively. For longer running videos, the scheduling of network resources becomes more complex because scheduling decisions last on the order of hours (and not minutes). The key to providing VCR functionality in these videos is the efficient use of the smoothing buffer.

5.2.2 Buffering Versus Delay

Using the a bandwidth smoothing algorithm for the delivery of stored video results in a trade-off between buffering and delay. To smooth large frame-size peaks such as those found at the end of the *Seminar* video (see Figure 5.1), the data in the burst must be prefetched before the peak is played back. Because VCR functionality is coupled

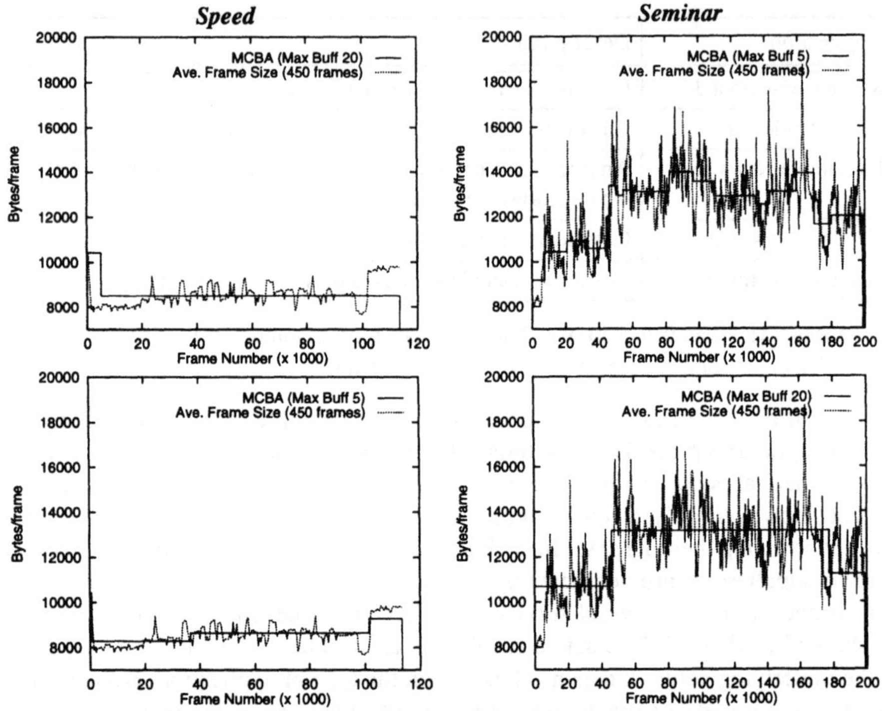

Figure 5.1: Bandwidth Smoothing Examples. This figure shows the plan created using the minimum changes bandwidth algorithm with a 20 MByte and 5 MByte buffer for the MJPEG encoded videos *Speed* and *Seminar.* The dashed lines represent the average frame sizes for 15 second (450 frame) groups within the videos.

with the buffering of frames, the burstiness exhibited by the videos impacts the ability to service VCR interactivity with buffering.

For our discussions, we will use the digitized movie *Speed* and the *Seminar* video. As shown in Figure 5.1, the bandwidth allocation plans generated by the MCBA algorithm result in very few required bandwidth changes for the playback of the videos. Recall, the bandwidth plans generated by algorithms such as the MCBA algorithm do not require any prefetching before the playback of the videos begin, hence, a high initial bandwidth may be required (as in the *Seminar* video). If the video request is made in advance, this initially high bandwidth requirement can be removed by prefetching data before the start of playback of the video. It is important to recall that the *Seminar* and *Speed* videos are Motion-JPEG encoded, thus, they do not take advantage of temporal similarities between frames. This results in buffering and bandwidth estimates that are conservative for the results shown. In general, using MPEG encoded video streams instead of Motion-JPEG encoded video streams results in one of two situations: 1) The actual buffer requirements are smaller than presented (assuming the same buffer residency times) or 2) The buffer residency times will be much higher

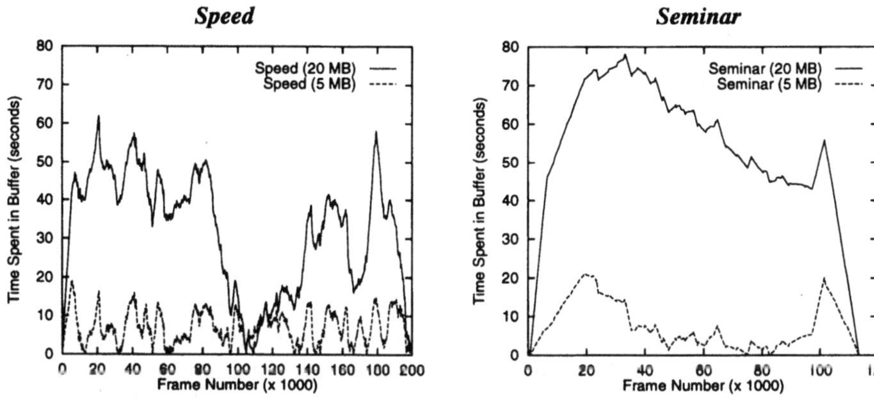

Figure 5.2: Buffer Residency Times. This figure shows the buffer residency times for the frames in the Motion-JPEG videos *Speed* and *Seminar* using a 5 and 20 MB buffer. For these videos and a 20 MB buffer, the average buffer residency time was 32.1 and 54.0 seconds for the *Speed* and *Seminar* videos, respectively. Note that for equivalent size buffers the residency times for MPEG encoded videos would be considerably larger.

than the numbers presented (assuming the same buffer sizes) because more frames can be prefetched with the same amount of buffer.With the use of MPEG's B and P frame types, the amount of buffering required to achieve the same amount of smoothing can be expected to be 4 to 10 times smaller.

Because algorithms such as the CBA, MCBA, and MVBA algorithms smooth bursts as much as possible through prefetching, the buffer residency times (the time that a frame sits in the buffer) can be fairly substantial. The buffer residency times for the videos *Speed* and *Seminar* using the optimal bandwidth allocation plans from Figure 5.1 are shown in Figure 5.2. As shown by Figure 5.2, the buffer residency times are correlated to the amount of buffering used for smoothing. That is, the larger the buffer used, the higher the buffer residency times tend to be. In addition, the variance of buffer residency times also depends on the long term burstiness of the video. As described in Figure 5.2, the amount of time a frame spends in the buffer can be on the order of half a minute to a minute for a 20 MB buffer. For the *Speed* video, there is a larger variation in frame sizes throughout the movie, resulting in buffer residency times that also vary more. For the *Seminar* video, the stream consists of roughly the same size frames except at the end where a larger bursts of frames occur. As a result, large buffer residency times are required to smooth out the large frame sizes at the end of the video. Incidentally, the end of the *Seminar* video consists of the lights turning on, a panning of the speaker toward the center of the room, and a short question and answer session that includes the first row of listeners.

The large buffer residency times introduced by non-window based smoothing techniques have a direct impact on the ability to provide users with VCR capabilities. If random access to any point is to be allowed (while keeping the video quality constant), the network may have to contend with a potentially large required burst in bandwidth above that originally allocated. This large burst of extra bandwidth may be required to make up for the absence of buffering (and delay) to help reduce the bandwidth requirements. Thus, providing VCR capabilities in a bandwidth smoothing environment can be a difficult task.

5.3 VCR Functionality

Any interactive video-on-demand system must bring together several interrelated issues such as scheduling of disk resources at the server, reserving underlying network bandwidth, and handling rate consumption changes. The support for VCR-functionality can be handled at several different layers. Most notably, a fair amount of work is focused on supporting VCR functions such as rewind-scan and fast-forward-scan at the server [CHEN94,DAN94a,DEYS94,SHEN95]. These systems assume that the delivery of data during the use of VCR functions is not buffered and is aimed at providing interactivity with frames being delivered from the server. While providing VCR functionality may ultimately require the server to run in this mode, it suffers from scalability problems from the overhead in the number of changing requests. On the other hand, for systems that deliver constant quality video and use bandwidth smoothing to reduce peak bandwidths, the bandwidth allocations (especially if made in advance) are somewhat rigid to change because of the buffer residency times needed to smooth bandwidth requirements. In this section, we describe a video-on-demand service that has several key features: constant quality video delivery and VCR functionality (with the *VCR-window*). Before describing the VCR-window, we first describe the type of interactivity that we expect to see in future video on demand systems.

5.3.1 VCR Interactivity

In a bandwidth-smoothing video-on-demand system, providing unconstrained full-function VCR capabilities can cause problems with the ability to deliver the required video data due to lack of network resources. By looking at the expected interactions during the playback of video, the video-on-demand system may be designed to take advantage of common interactions. For video-on-demand services, we believe that video-on-demand users typically change the access pattern during the playback of a video that fall into one of the four categories:

- *Pause/Stop* - The user stops the movie for a short time to answer a phone call, go to the kitchen, etc.
- *Rewind* - The user rewinds the video to play back part of the video that was not understand
- *Examine* - The user stops the VCR to examine more closely a portion of the video. As an example, a user may be watching a football game

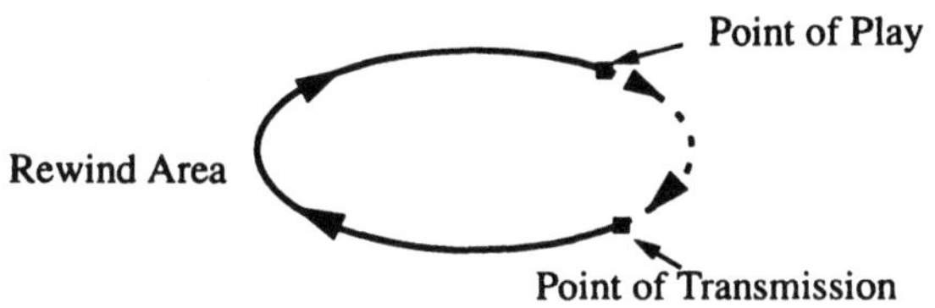

Figure 5.3: Circular Buffer Example. This figure shows the conceptual model of buffering for video data. The point of play (POP) and the point of transmission (POT) move clockwise. The solid line represents the rewind area, while the dashed line represents the amount of buffering that is in use for prefetching (smoothing)

and wants to see a certain play a couple of times in slow motion to see why it did or didn't work.

- *Fast forward scan* - The user scans past parts of the video such as commercials in the program.

In the future, we believe that users may also require all of these functions from a video-on-demand system, although the actual distribution of access patterns within these categories may change. As an example, consider the operation fast-forward scan, which typically gets used to fast-forward through commercials. As mentioned earlier, it is unclear how commercials will play a role in future video-on-demand systems. Nevertheless, we should not rule out the possibility of fast-forward scans in our discussion. We expect, however, that many of the accesses will be in a localized area within the video where a limited window of full function VCR capabilities may suffice. In addition, by limiting the window size, the network bandwidth reservation levels may not need to be altered, and the required interactions with servers and networks may be minimized.

5.3.2 The VCR-window

To allow for VCR functionality, we propose a different model of video delivery which allows users to have full function VCR controls in a limited window called the *VCR-window.* In our model of video transfer, we allow all VCR functions to occur at any time within the course of playback but limit the range of accessible data without having to renegotiate the reserved bandwidth. We define the notion of the point of play (POP) to be the furthest frame in the video that has been viewed by the user and the point of transmission (POT) as the furthest frame in the movie that resides in the client buffer. Our model then consists of viewing the smoothing buffer as a circular buffer, in which, the POP and POT traverse the circumference in a clock-wise manner (see Figure 5.3). The distance the POT is ahead of the POP is the amount of buffer space used for prefetching. The remaining part of the circumference, the *rewind area*, is the amount of data that has been played back and is still in the buffer. Thus, when the buffer is nearly full, the POT is just behind the POP, and when the buffer is nearly empty, the POP is just behind the POT. Note, if the POT ever passes the POP or the POP passes the POT, we have buffer overflow and buffer underflow, respectively.

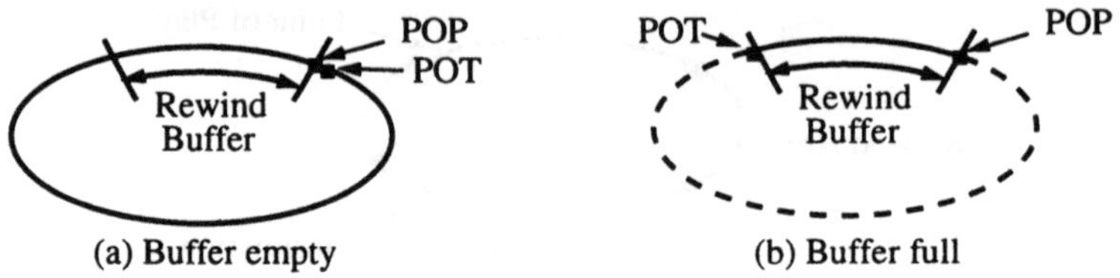

Figure 5.4: Buffer Limit Conditions. Figures (a) and (b) show the cases that occur during playback when the buffer is empty and full, respectively. The solid line represents data that has been played back but not removed from the buffer, while the dashed line represents data that has been transmitted but not played back.

Using these definitions of the POT and POP, we make the observation that we can allow the user to have full function VCR capabilities in the area that the POP leads the POT without changing the bandwidth reservation level. No change in bandwidth is required because the data that is being viewed is sitting in the buffer already. One major drawback of this method is that when the buffer is nearly full the POP does not lead the POT by any significant amount. To ensure that the rewind area has some minimum amount of data, we define the *rewind buffer* to be the closest distance that the POT can approach the POP. For clarity we still refer to the total distance that the POP leads the POT as the *rewind area* (or the VCR-window). Figure 5.4 shows the resulting two cases when the buffer is full and empty for the VCR-window.

Formally, we can define the amount of available data in the rewind area on the ith frame as

$$RewBuffSize(i) = MaxBuff - \left(\left(\sum_{j=0}^{i} BwAlloc(j)\right) - \left(\sum_{j=0}^{i} FrameSize(j)\right)\right)$$

where,

- *MaxBuff* is the maximum buffer size including the *Rewind Buffer.*
- *BwAlloc(k)* is the bandwidth allocation on frame k. Note, we assume that the bandwidth allocation plan is allocated in bytes/frame.
- *FrameSize(k)* is the frame size of the kth frame.

This equation takes the difference between the total bandwidth received and the total bandwidth played back (i.e. the amount of data in the buffer) and subtracts it from the amount of buffering available. This equation does not, however, calculate the amount of video that is actually available but calculates its aggregate size. We can calculate the additional amount of rewind buffer needed to have T frames available in the buffer on the ith frame as

$$AddBuffReq(i, T) = \left(\sum_{k=max(0, i-T)}^{i} FrameSize(k)\right) - RewBuffSize(i)$$

This equation is essentially the size of the T frames needed in the rewind area with the amount of data already in the rewind area subtracted. If the user requires that 100% of

Figure 5.5: VCR-Window Example. This figure shows the adjustment in the bandwidth allocation plan that is made when a user uses the VCR controls for i time units (include the time to get pack to the POP that it was at). The remaining portion of the bandwidth allocation plan is then shifted by the amount of time spent in the rewind area. In this case, it is shifted i time units.

the time the buffer has T frames in it, then the additional amount of buffering needed is simply the maximum AddBuffReq() over all frames within the movie. That is, to ensure the buffer *always* has T frames in the minimum buffer requirement *MinBuffReq(T)* is:

$$MinBuffReq(T) = \max_{T \le j \le N} AddBuffReq(j, T)$$

To allow for VCR capabilities, when a user starts moving in the rewind area, the data flow from the server is stopped. The flow is then restarted only when the playback point reaches the POP again. Thus, only two interactions to the server and network are required to support the VCR-window, one to stop the data flow, and one to start the data flow again. Because the delivery of bandwidth starts at exactly the same point at which the data was stopped, no changes in the bandwidth reservation level are necessary while allowing for a window of full function VCR capabilities. For long term bandwidth reservations, the only modification necessary is the extension of the bandwidth requirement by the amount of time that was spent in the rewind area. Using this model for VCR functionality, the operations stop/pause, rewind, and examine can be provided to users with only minimal interaction with the network and server. As an example, consider the bandwidth allocation plan shown in Figure 5.5. At timc t, the user decides to stop the playback and examine the video that was just played. Suppose that the total time it takes for the user to examine the video and get back to time t in the video is i time units. We then move all bandwidth allocations after the time t in the original bandwidth allocation plan to start at time t', the time at which playback started again. Note, by shifting the bandwidth allocation plan after time t by i time units, the resultant bandwidth reservation has been modified. We discuss how the reservation scheme can be modified to handle this change later in this chapter.

5.3.3 Access Outside the VCR window

Scans to points outside the VCR window require renegotiations with the network and server. For long fast-forwards, the consumption rate originally anticipated will now be compressed in time, resulting in the need for more bandwidth than was originally planned for, assuming all the frames are delivered. We expect that these interactions may not occur very frequently, nonetheless, they should not be disallowed. For the renegotiation of bandwidth reservations in these cases, we expect that the notion of *contingency channels* which reserve part of the network capacity to handle changes in consumption rate are useful [DAN94]. Because the VCR-window filters many of the interactions that are required through the use of buffering, the contingency channels can be more efficiently allocated to handling the special cases that may arise during the playback of video.

Our work on contingency channels is derived from the work at IBM on batching of the delivery of video data for clients watching the same movie with the same approximate playback times [DAN94]. In their work, the authors consider the use of pause/resume functions for the VCR controls on how multiple channels can be batched together, hence, the contingency channels are only used to "unbatch" a client that has paused the video and is not temporally close enough to the channel it was originally batched with. The "unbatched" client is then re-batched with possibly a different group of clients watching the same movie at about the same playback time. The actual bandwidth allocation for the movie, however, is not addressed in this work as well as the use of any buffering that may be used to smooth bandwidth requests. As a result of this, the contingency channel may be used by a client for a short time or for a very long time depending on where the playback time of other batched users is.

For our purposes, we use the contingency channel in a slightly different manner. We do not consider batching of movie channels but use the idea of setting aside bandwidth for the occasional accesses that are made outside of the VCR-window and only use the contingency channel for providing VCR functionality and not batching. Therefore, the contingency channel in our work is used by clients for a short amount of time until their bandwidth requirements reach a level that is within their originally agreed upon bandwidth reservations.

For accesses outside the VCR-window, it is important to get the bandwidth consumption rate for the clients back to their original bandwidth reservations as soon as possible. By returning the system back to its steady state as soon as possible, the network manager needs to only worry about scheduling the contingency channel part of the access outside of the VCR-window (as opposed to re-admitting the entire bandwidth plan). As an example, consider the optimal bandwidth allocation delivery plan shown in Figure 5.6 that has a point to be randomly accessed. Ideally, an impulse of data would be issued at the point of random access and the bandwidth requirements would then fall below the bandwidth requirements for the entire original bandwidth plan immediately. Because impulses of data are not possible, a plan for the use of the contingency channel must be created. For this random access at point PT_{access}, let BW_{new} be the critical bandwidth from PT_{access} *with no bytes in the buffer.* In addition, let $Bytes_{behind}$ be the difference between $F_{low}(PT_{access})$ and the buffer occupancy of the original bandwidth plan at PT_{access}. Then, we note that any bandwidth greater than BW_{new} does not cause buffer starvation and that once $Bytes_{behind}$ have been delivered

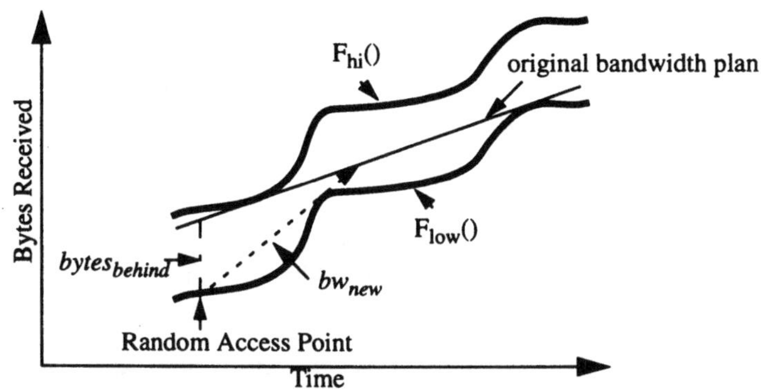

Figure 5.6: Random Access and Smoothing. This figure shows the handling of accesses to a random location within a video delivery plan. The dashed vertical line shows the necessary amount of data required to be sent via the contingency channel. The minimum amount of bandwidth necessary is determined by the critical bandwidth starting from the random access point with 0 bytes in the buffer. Once the plan reaches the original allocation, the contingency channel for that client can be freed.

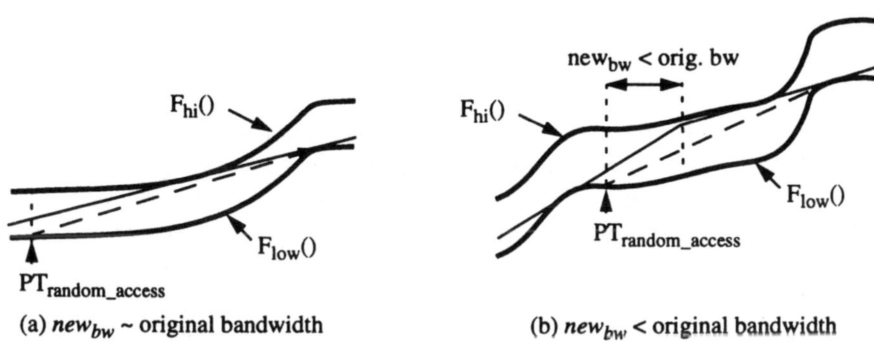

Figure 5.7: Critical Bandwidths and Random Starting Points. In these figures, thin solid lines are the original bandwidth allocations, while the dashed lines are the critical bandwidths starting from PT_{random_access}. Figure (a) shows an example starting point where the bandwidth requirement for the contingency channel is nearly the same as the original bandwidth allocation, while Figure (b) shows an example starting point where the bandwidth requirement for the random starting point is less than the actual original bandwidth allocation plan.

the contingency channel can then be freed.

For access to random starting points outside of the VCR-window, the critical bandwidth is generally larger than the original bandwidth allocation at that point. It is, however, entirely possible that the critical bandwidth from the random starting point is nearly the same as (or even below) the original bandwidth allocation at the random point. As an example consider, the two examples shown in Figure 5.7. In

Figure 5.7(a), the critical bandwidth is nearly the same as the original plan. Because the runs in the optimal bandwidth allocation algorithm can run in the tens of minutes, the actual difference in bandwidth requirement may be very small. Figure 5.7(b) shows an example where the critical bandwidth is actually below the bandwidth at the random access point.

In general, the accesses that are made to points outside of the VCR-window are expected to be in the vicinity of the playback point. As a result, the data in the buffer may still be usable, thereby reducing the actual bandwidth requirement from the contingency channel.

Contingency Channel Allocation - An allocation back-off approach

Implementing the contingency channel poses an interesting problem - *how should the contingency channel bandwidth be allocated?* For the random access that is shown in Figure 5.6 and Figure 5.7, any bandwidth greater than the bw_{new} will work. Thus, a trade-off between using all of the bandwidth of the contingency channel for a shorter period of time, or allocating at the critical bandwidth bw_{new} and using the contingency channel for a longer period of time must be made. The former allows the contingency channel to be freed as soon as possible, but risks starving other outstanding requests. The latter approach may not make the best use of bandwidth available on the contingency channel. To balance between these goals we propose an *allocation back-off strategy* for the allocation of the contingency channel.

The *allocation back-off strategy* allocates the entire available contingency channel bandwidth to a single client when no other clients require servicing. When another request arrives, the network manager picks one (or more) of the users to decrease its bandwidth requirement either in half or to its critical bandwidth to allow the new user to use the contingency channel to re-synchronize its bandwidth allocation plan. When a client is done with its contingency channel allocation, the network manager then notifies one of the clients to increase its use of the contingency channel. By allocating the contingency channel in this manner, the network manager can make the most use of its contingency channel bandwidth, while assuring users a reasonable response time. In the event that the contingency channel is entirely allocated, a user may need to start the retrieval of bandwidth at a smaller rate (thus delaying the actual start-up of the video). With the filtering provided by the VCR-window, we expect that the number of times that the contingency channel reaches capacity and cannot handle other requests will be fairly rare.

5.4 An In-Advance Reservation Scheme

Resource reservations are an important part of network management for both in-advance and on the fly reservations because the network can then accurately estimate the bandwidth requirements of the clients. For stored video-on-demand services, the ability to provide reservations of bandwidth in advance can make the job of resource

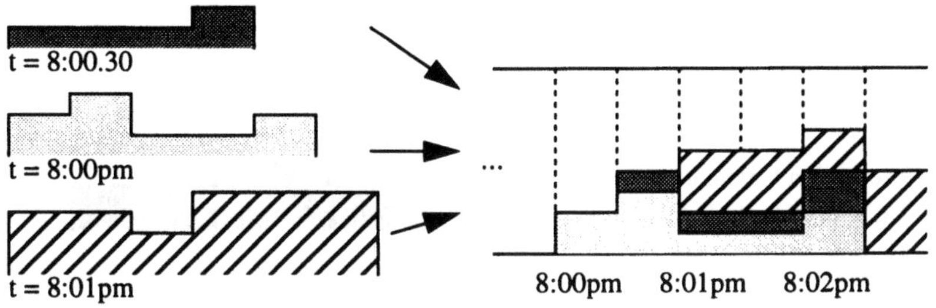

Figure 5.8: Resource Reservation Scheme. This figure shows the reservation of bandwidth for three sample streams. Bandwidth is reserved in 30 second intervals to reduce fragmentation of bandwidth.

allocation easier[LITT94]. Resource reservation schemes have two key components that are necessary for resource reservations: the bandwidth requirement and the duration that the bandwidth requirement is needed [DEGE95,FERR95,WOLF95]. Without providing these, resource reservations in-advance then becomes a difficult task. In addition, Ferrari, Gupta, and Ventre point out that scheduling of bandwidth based on some fixed interval reduces the fragmentation that the reservation scheme has to contend with[FERR95]. Finally, it is commonly agreed upon that advance reservations will consist of two distinct phases, an admission control phase where the reservation is admitted and an enforcement phase where the bandwidth allocation is enforced.

Our in-advance reservation model is a slotted reservation scheme with a minimum bandwidth allocation slot of 30 seconds. The user machine/set-top-box creates a bandwidth allocation plan based on the slot boundaries and then passes this plan to the server and network for admission control. The network managers then compare the bandwidth requirements of the new channel and compare it to the available bandwidth allocation plan offered by the user. The example in Figure 5.8 shows sample requests that may be sent to the network manager. By using 30 second bandwidth allocation slots, the network manager only needs to evaluate 180 slots for a 90 minute video, reducing the complexity of the admission control algorithm. The network manager then allocates the available resources to the new channel if available. If the available bandwidth does not exist, then the network manager can either 1) offer a new starting time which can satisfy the bandwidth allocation plan or 2) create a different network path to the server which can satisfy the request.

Passing bandwidth plans to the network manager as part of admission control creates rigid schedules. To allow VCR-window functionality, the resource reservation system must reserve bandwidth based on the maximum amount of "VCR-time" to be introduced by the viewer. The total time that the video can be delayed must be declared at admission control. The actual amount of VCR-time delay reserved depends on the guarantees that the user expects and the quality of service expected if the delay bounds are exceeded. The amount of VCR-time reserved may be also determined by economic factors (i.e. how much users are willing to pay for bandwidth that they may

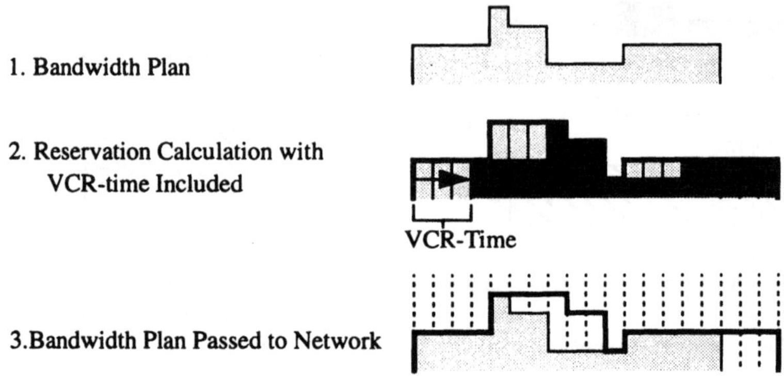

Figure 5.9: Bandwidth Reservation Calculation. 1) Bandwidth plan creation. 2) Client machine creates second plan that incorporates "VCR-Time" in the plan. 3) The VCR-time calculated bandwidth is passed to the network and server as part of admission control. This plan is denoted by the heavy solid line.

not use). For now, we assume the worst case for this delay, in that, all of the delay can occur at any interval. Therefore, in the calculation of the bandwidth allocation plan used for admission control, we create a bandwidth allocation plan that reserves the data such that at each point within the movie the video can be stopped for the maximum delay. Let *T* be the delay (in frames) for VCR functionality that is required from the user and *BwPlan(i)* be the bandwidth requirement on frame *i*. Then the new bandwidth allocation plan (in bytes/frame) can be defined as

$$NewBwPlan(i) = \max_{i - T \le j \le i} BwPlan(j)$$

Figure 5.9 shows a sample bandwidth allocation plan calculation that has the expected VCR-induced delay built into the bandwidth allocation plan.

5.5 Experimentation

The success of the VCR-window concept depends on how much data is available in the rewind area at any given time as well as the amount of buffering required for use as the rewind buffer. As the amount of buffering devoted to the rewind buffer increases, the amount of smoothing available diminishes. The success of the reservation system depends on the effectiveness of the video-on-demand system to utilize its bandwidth. In order to fully understand the impact of buffering on the VCR-window and the associated in-advance reservation system, we have digitized 17 full-length movies along with 3 seminars that were presented at the University of Michigan. For the experiments, we used the MCBA algorithm with prefetching on the initial run.

5.5.1 VCR-window Experimentation

In this section, we examine the amount of data available in the *VCR-window* under

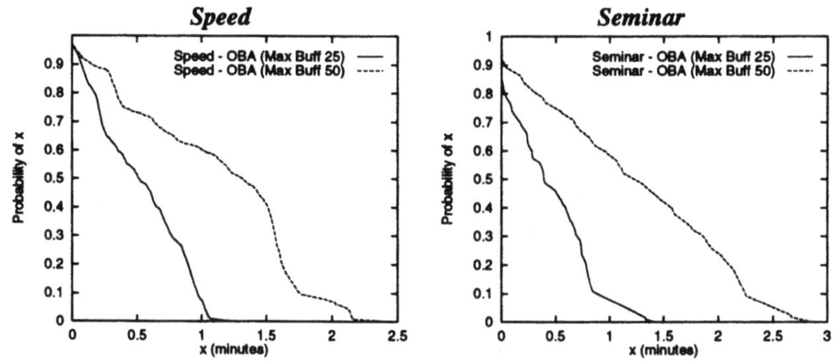

Figure 5.10: Buffer Rewind Probabilities. These graphs show for a given amount of time, *x*, the probability that *x* amount of video is available in the rewind area without renegotiation and with the rewind buffer set to 0. For 25 and 50 Mbyte buffers, this results in having 30 seconds of video available 52.8% and 75.3% of the time, respectively, for the video *Speed*. Similarly, the *Seminar* video had 30 seconds of video available 46.9% and 77.9% of the time, respectively.

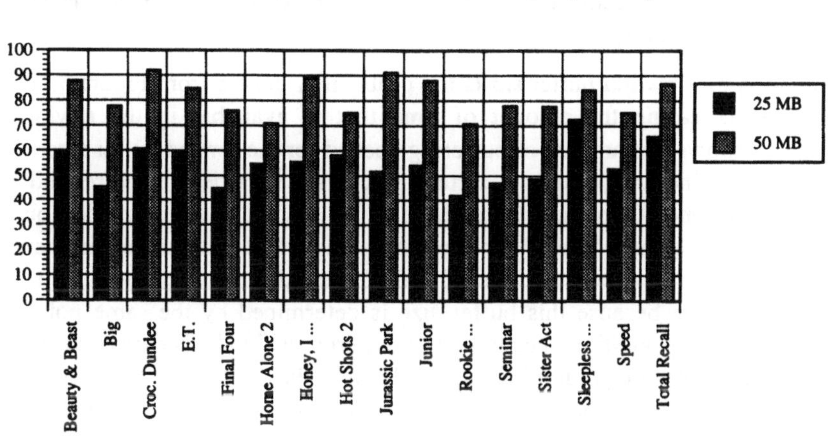

Figure 5.11: Buffer Rewind Times for all Movies. This figure shows the percentage of time that rewind area contains more than 30 seconds of video for the 25 and 50 MByte smoothing buffer with the rewind buffer size set to 0.

bandwidth smoothing. Figure 5.10 shows for a given amount of time, *x*, the probability that *x* amount of video data is available in the rewind area with the rewind buffer size set to 0. For the *Speed* video, using a 25 MByte buffer results in over half a minute of video in the rewind area 53% of the time while using a 50 MByte buffer results in over half a minute of video in the rewind area 75% of the time. In addition, 15 seconds of video is available 74% and 91% of the time for the 25 and 50 Mbyte buffers. The *Seminar* video exhibits similar numbers to the *Speed* video. As shown in Figure 5.11, the percentage of time that the rewind area contains more than 30 seconds of video for the rest of the videos exhibits similar numbers as well. Typically, the

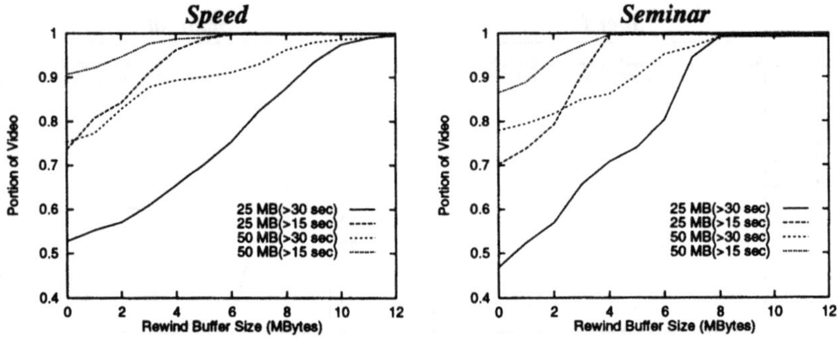

Figure 5.12: Buffer Rewind Size Requirements. These figures show the rewind buffer size requirement necessary to ensure that some percentage of the time, the VCR-window has 15 and 30 seconds of video in it for the movie *Speed.* As an example, with a 25 MByte smoothing buffer, in order to achieve 15 seconds of buffering 90% of the time, roughly 3MBytes of rewind buffer is required above the 25 MByte smoothing buffer.

25 and 50 MB buffers results in the rewind area with 30 seconds of video 45-60% and 75-90% of the time, respectively.

The addition of a rewind buffer shifts the probability curves from Figure 5.10 to the right, thus increasing the amount of time that is available in the rewind area. Figure 5.12 shows, the amount of buffering needed for the rewind buffer size in order to have the rewind area contain a certain percentage of video in the rewind buffer greater than 15 and 30 seconds. Note, these buffer rewind sizes are in addition to the 25 and 50 MByte buffers used for the smoothing of bandwidth requirements. As expected the lines for the same time (15 and 30 seconds) approach the same required rewind buffer size because this buffer size is determined by the same point (area) within the video. In addition, the amount of required rewind buffer space decreases as the size of the smoothing buffer increases. This is mainly due to the larger buffer sizes having more rewind area on average. In order to achieve at least 15 seconds of video in the rewind area 95% of the time, the movie *Speed* requires only 4 and 2 MBytes of rewind buffer for the 25 and 50 MByte smoothing buffers, respectively. The *Seminar* video approaches the 100% line faster than the *Speed* video. This is due to the smaller (and more constant) average bit rate of the *Seminar* versus the *Speed* video. If we take the average frame sizes for the videos and multiply it by the number of frames in 30 seconds of video (900 frames), the *Speed* video results in 11.1 MB while the *Seminar* video results in 7.7 MB. It is interesting to note that these videos approach 100% near these values.

Figure 5.13 shows the percentage of time that 30 seconds of movie is available when using an 8 MByte rewind buffer. The highest bit rate video *Final Four* results in the smallest percentage of rewind times greater than 30 seconds, while the 3 smallest bit rate videos (*E.T., Crocodile Dundee,* and *Sleepless in Seattle*) result in the highest percentage of rewind times. This suggests that the rewind size is roughly correlated to

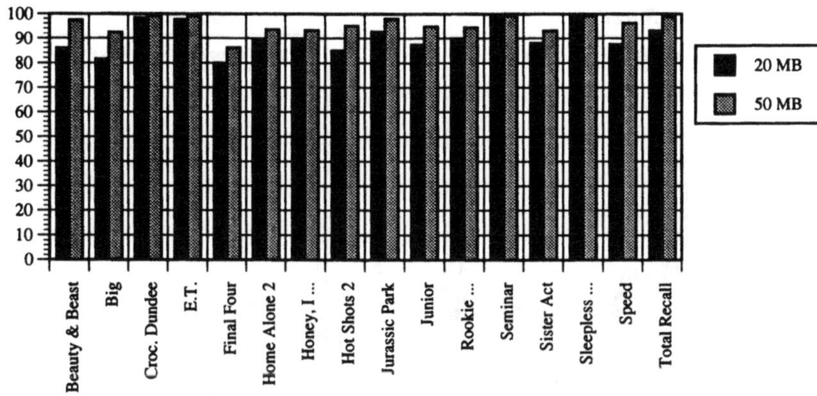

Figure 5.13: Buffer Rewind Sizes for All Movies. This figure shows the percentage of time that 30 seconds of video is available using an 8 MByte rewind buffer in addition to the 25 and 50 MByte smoothing buffer.

the average bit rate that the encoded movie has. Thus, we expect that the use of tighter encoding schemes such as MPEG with B and P frames reduces the overall requirement of the rewind buffer size.

5.5.2 Accesses Outside the VCR-window

The use of contingency channels to serve requests outside of the VCR-window should not occur that frequently, however, if a user accesses an area outside of the VCR-window, the contingency channel needs to provide bandwidth for the client to return to its originally agreed upon reservation. To show the expected resource requirements for random accesses outside of the VCR-window, we assume that the network link layer is a 100 Mbit/sec link and that only 5% of the link (i.e. 5Mbits/sec) is reserved for the contingency channel. For accesses outside of the VCR-window, we then graphed the time required for resynchronization using the entire contingency channel bandwidth. as well as the re-synchronization time at the critical bandwidth. Because the critical bandwidth can be approximately the same or lower than the original bandwidth allocation, we force the minimum contingency allocation to be at least 90 kbytes/sec, which is approximately one quarter the average bit rate of the videos that we have digitized and approximately 14% of the contingency channel capacity. This avoids excessively long re-synchronization times due to a very small difference in the original bandwidth allocation and the critical bandwidth from the starting point.

Figure 5.14 shows the re-synchronization times for the videos *Speed* and *Seminar*. The re-synchronization times using the entire contingency channel are on the order of half a minute for both movies. For contingency channels that have twice as much bandwidth, the graph for the contingency channel at the maximum bandwidth is scaled in half. As shown by the graphs, the contingency times at the minimum are directly related to the amount of data in the buffer that need to be made up. As a

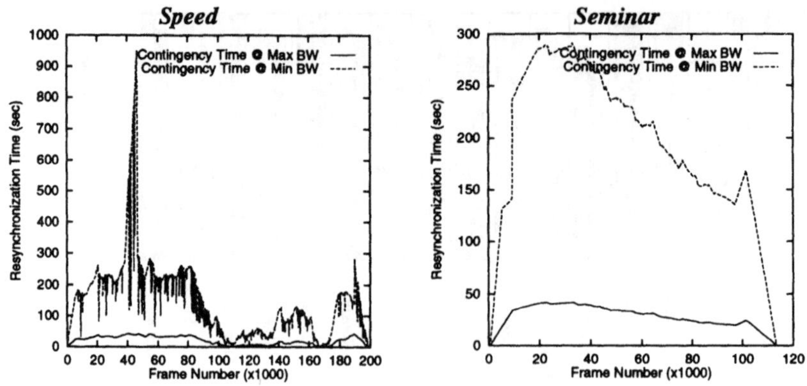

Figure 5.14: Random Access Times for Contingency Channel Usage. This figure shows the resynchronization time required for the bandwidth usage of a random access to return to the originally allocated bandwidth (using a 25 MB smoothing buffer and the MCBA algorithm). The solid lines represent the time required for re-synchronization using the entire bandwidth of a 5Mbit/sec contingency channel. The dotted lines show the re-synchronization times for allocating the bandwidth of the contingency channel at the critical bandwidth from the random starting point or at 90kbytes/sec, which ever is higher.

result, the graphs for the contingency times are very similar to the buffer occupancy graphs in Figure 5.2.

Accesses just outside of the VCR-window may be able to take advantage of data that is already sitting in the buffer, thereby, reducing the amount of resources required from the contingency channel. The reduction of contingency channel resources is, of course, directly related to what data is buffered and where the new point of play is. In Figure 5.15, we have graphed the contingency channel usage for forward accesses 10 seconds outside of the VCR-window. As shown, by the graphs, the average amount of time needed to re-synchronize with the original bandwidth allocations is much smaller than random accesses (as in Figure 5.14). As an example, the videos *Speed* and *Seminar* need, on average, 4 and 6 seconds of the entire contingency channel bandwidth to re-synchronize with the original bandwidth plans. The sharp peak in the contingency times for the movie speed results from an increase in bandwidth in the original bandwidth allocation plan. The increase in bandwidth is almost the same as the critical bandwidth from the starting point, resulting a very long contingency channel time. Allocating the contingency channel at its maximum bandwidth, however, removes this spike.

5.5.3 Bandwidth Reservations

For bandwidth reservations, one of the main concerns is the actual network utilization versus the amount of bandwidth that was allocated. For example, if the amount of bandwidth reserved is around 95% but only 50% of the bandwidth is actually used,

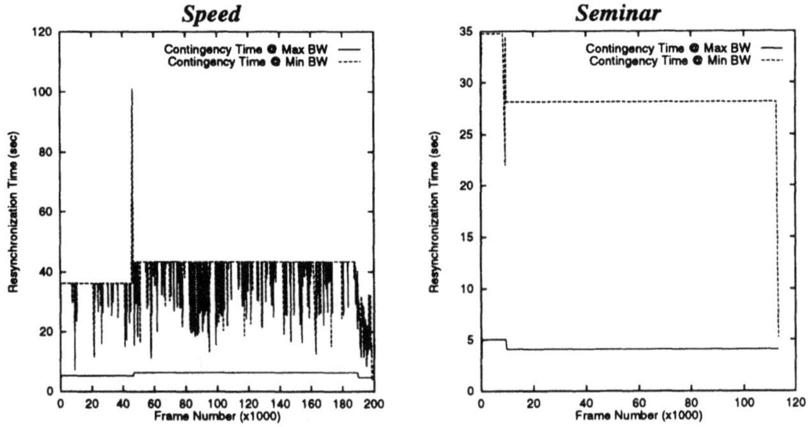

Figure 5.15: Contingency Channel Usage for Local Accesses. This figure shows the resynchronization time required for the bandwidth usage of accesses that are 10 seconds outside of the VCR-window (using a 25 MB smoothing buffer and the MCBA algorithm). The solid lines represent the time required for re-synchronization using the entire bandwidth of a 5Mbit/sec contingency channel. The dotted lines show the re-synchronization times for allocating the bandwidth of the contingency channel at the critical bandwidth from the random starting point or at 90kbytes/sec, which ever is higher.

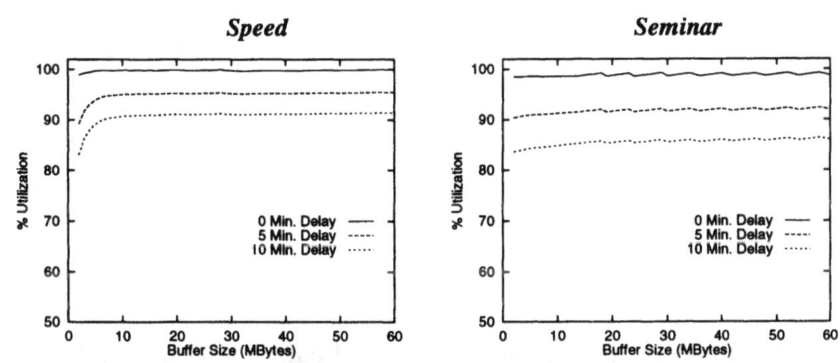

Figure 5.16: Reservation Utilization. These graphs show the reservation utilization for the video *Speed* and *Seminar* with reservations made on a 30 second period and reserved with the maximum additional delay expected during playback.

then the reservation scheme may need to be modified to be more effective in utilizing the network. As shown in Figure 5.16, the reservations based on a 30 second period with no extra delay built into the reservation plan for VCR functionality yield reservation utilizations between 99% and 100% of what was reserved. Thus, the MCBA allocation (with prefetching on the first run) yields bandwidth allocation plans that utilize nearly all the bandwidth reserved based on 30 second periods and suffers very little internal fragmentation of bandwidth allocations. Furthermore, the utilizations can be

Figure 5.17: Peak Bandwidth Reservations. The heavy solid line shows the creation of a peak bandwidth allocation plan. This bandwidth allocation plan is used for the advanced reservations made in Figure 5.18.

increased by aligning bandwidth change boundaries with the slot boundaries. Three trends are worth noting in Figure 5.16. First, for very small buffer sizes (< 5 MB), the utilization is hurt by two things, more bandwidth changes that are not aligned with slot boundaries and more bandwidth is reserved due to the limitation of the prefetch buffer in smoothing bandwidth requests. Second, because the utilization for the MCBA algorithm is quite high, the utilization for the streams reach their limits fairly quickly. Finally, the *Seminar* video has lower utilization for the 5 and 10 minute delays because the video is shorter in length, thus, the 5 and 10 minute delay reservations make up a larger portion of their reservations. With tighter encoding mechanisms, the utilization can be expected to be higher with no other modifications to the buffer size or delay for VCR functionality.

The expected overall utilization of the network is not captured by the graphs in Figure 5.16 because they do not capture the peak reservations which may affect other bandwidth allocation plans. To establish a "lower bound" on the expected network utilization, we have modified the bandwidth allocation plans to have both the peak bandwidth reservation for the *entire* video and the expected VCR induced delay. A sample graph allocation is shown in Figure 5.17. As a result, the peak bandwidth allocation makes the reservation for the *entire* movie as one constant bandwidth reservation. We then graphed the expected bandwidth utilization based on these peak bandwidth allocations instead of the bandwidth reservations described in Section 5.4. As shown by Figure 5.18, we see that the bandwidth utilization has dropped from those shown in Figure 5.16. The bandwidth utilizations, however, are still reasonable. Using a 25 MByte smoothing buffer, no rewind buffer, and an extra 5 minutes of delay in the bandwidth reservations, the movie *Speed* has a utilization of 90.7% while the *Seminar* video has a utilization of 92.7%. Thus, even for peak bandwidth reservations with 5 extra minutes reserved, we expect that the bandwidth utilization can be held fairly high. The peak bandwidth reservations do not affect the *Seminar* video as much as the *Speed* video because it has less variation between frame sizes resulting in smaller peaks when they occur.

Finally, Figure 5.19 and Figure 5.20 show the normal reservation utilizations and peak reservations utilizations in the same exact way that Figure 5.16 and Figure 5.18 were made, respectively. In Figure 5.19, the normal reservation scheme with an additional 5 minute delay for both 25 and 50 MByte buffers are shown for all movies.

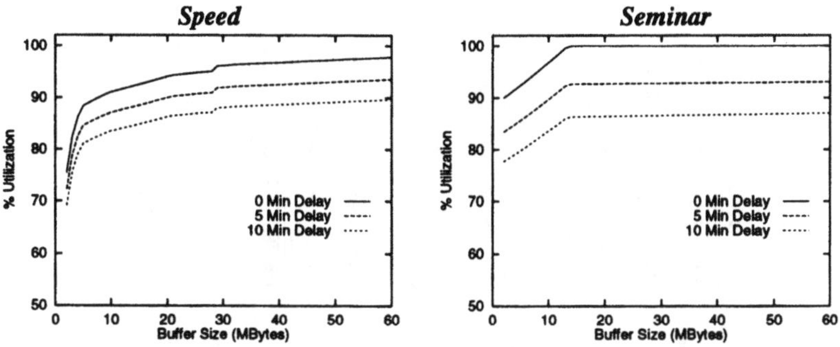

Figure 5.18: Peak Reservation Utilization. These graphs show the peak reservation utilization for the video *Speed* and *Seminar* with reservations made at the peak bandwidth allocation and with the maximum additional delay expected during playback.

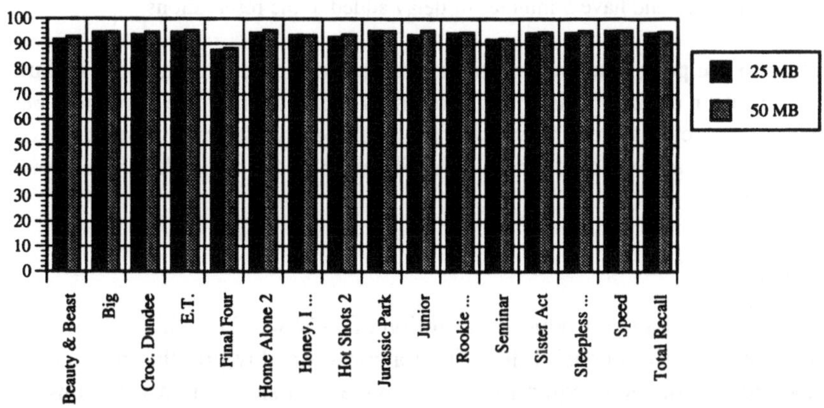

Figure 5.19: Reservation Utilization for Other Video Data. This figure shows the reservation utilization for bandwidth plans that are allocated in 30 second periods and have 5 minutes of delay added to the reservations. All utilizations were in the 90% to 95% range with the exception of the *Final Four* video.

They result in utilization ranging from 90% to 95% with the exception of the *Final Four* video. This result is expected as the *Final Four* video is only 41 minutes in length, thus, the extra 5 minutes accounts for 11% of the video. As expected the peak utilizations are generally less than the normal reservation method. In addition, the 25MB buffers are affected more because they cannot remove the peak burstiness as much as with a 50 MB buffer. Nonetheless, they exhibit fairly good utilizations. The video *Beauty and the Beast* video is affected the most by using a peak bandwidth reservation. The reason this occurs is that a peak of very large frame sizes could not be overcome with smoothing in a small area within the movie. We expect that these singular peaks may be scheduled to fit into the valleys of other bandwidth allocation reservations. Some movies exhibit no change in utilization from the reservation

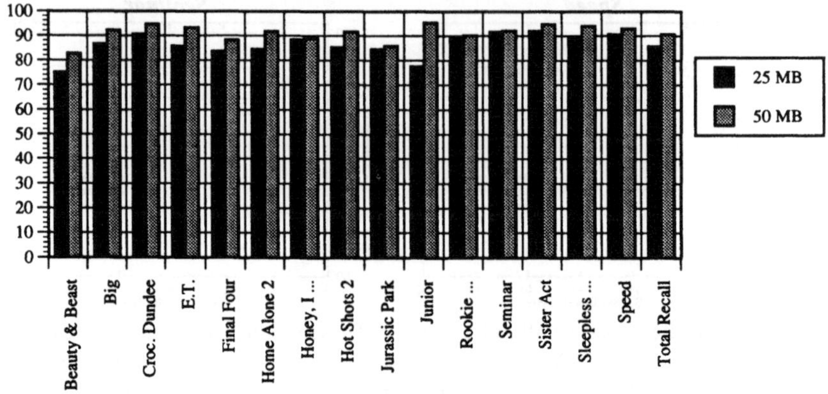

Figure 5.20: Peak Reservation Utilization for Other Video Data. This figure shows the peak reservation utilization for bandwidth plans that are allocated in 30 second periods and have 5 minutes of delay added to the reservations.

utilization to the peak reservation utilization. In these cases, the amount of buffering in the reservation utilization is enough to remove almost all of the burstiness and thus does not get affected as much by using the peak bandwidth requirement. In general, however, the overall expected bandwidth utilization of the network can be expected to be fairly high.

5.6 Summary

In this chapter, we have introduced the notion of *VCR-window* which allows a user to have full function VCR capabilities within a constrained region that does not change the bandwidth allocation requirements. We have also shown that providing 30 seconds of video available for 90% of the time can be implemented with a small amount of additional buffering, even for loosely encoded Motion-JPEG video. We expect that the majority of interactions that occur during the playback of video can be accounted for by using this technique. For users who want a guarantee of some amount of video *always* available in the rewind area, the required rewind buffer size is determined by a few scenes within the movie. For users who are willing to settle for lesser guarantees during the examine or scan phases, the VCR functionality can always be provided by the server which can fit the required video into the reserved channel capacity. Work on supporting scan operations from the server can be found in [CHEN94, DEYS94, SHEN95], while modifying compressed video to fit within a specified channel capacity can be found in [PANC92, PANC93].

We have also presented a slotted, in-advance resource reservation scheme to be used in conjunction with the VCR-window. The optimal bandwidth allocation algorithm results in very high network bandwidth utilization even under periodic scheduling boundaries. This is mainly due to the optimal bandwidth allocation algorithm minimizing the number of bandwidth changes as well as the peak required bandwidth. Nonetheless, the total amount of smoothing available depends on the long-term burstiness of the data itself. Using the advance reservation scheme in conjunction with the optimal bandwidth allocation algorithm allows users to have 5 to 10 minutes of "VCR-time" without degenerating the utilization. We expect that the lower bound for network utilization to be at least 80 percent. The 5 to 10 minutes of extra reserved "VCR-time" can be allocated for users to browse commercials or previews of other movies, assuming that they fit into the bandwidth reservation or are viewed at a slightly lower quality.

In the event more "random" access patterns are required such as jumps or scans of more than a couple of minutes in the video are required, renegotiation of bandwidth most likely is required or the reservation of bandwidth with that is a lot higher than actually used. The size and magnitude of these contingency channels depends on the percentage of times that the users in the video-on-demand system stray from the VCR-window. While we expect that the frequency of these occurrences to be quite small, the video-on-demand system should provide this flexibility. Our results indicate that allocating as little as 5 Mbits/sec of contingency channel can allow users that make local accesses outside of the VCR-window to re-synchronize with their original bandwidth allocation plans within a few seconds. These times are expected to be even smaller with tighter encoding of the video. Finally, for random accesses, the use of indexing schemes to allow access at distinct points within a video may allow the bandwidth requirements to be handled in a more efficient manner for accesses outside the VCR window.

6

BANDWIDTH SMOOTHING FOR INTERACTIVITY

6.1 Introduction

As we have studied in the last chapter, the use of bandwidth smoothing algorithms complicate the ability to provide fully interactive functions. For accesses outside of the *VCR-window*, minimizing the amount of data sitting in the client buffer can aid in reducing the amount of bandwidth required when long searches outside of the VCR window are invoked. In this chapter, we present a class of bandwidth smoothing techniques that may be more appropriate for interactive video-on-demand systems.

We first present the *rate-constrained bandwidth smoothing* which, given a maximum rate constraint, results in a bandwidth smoothing plan that has the minimum buffer utilization and uses the minimum-maximum buffer size of any delivery plan that adheres to the rate constraint. While the rate-constrained bandwidth smoothing (RCBS) algorithm results in the minimum buffer utilization (for a particular rate constraint), it typically creates plans that require orders of magnitude more rate changes than algorithms such as the critical bandwidth allocation algorithm.

To take advantage of smaller buffer residency times as well as the advantages that bandwidth smoothing approaches like the critical bandwidth allocation algorithm have to offer, we introduce the notion of *time-constrained bandwidth smoothing.* Specifically, we propose two new algorithms, a *time-constrained bandwidth smoothing algorithm* and a *rate/time constrained bandwidth smoothing*. By using a maximum buffer residency time, t, as a parameter in the creation of the bandwidth plans, these algorithms allow for the advantages of small buffer residency times *as well as* smoothing the number of bandwidth changes that are required for continuous playback. The time-constrained bandwidth smoothing algorithm takes two parameters, a maximum prefetch time t and a maximum buffer size b. The algorithm then creates a plan for the continuous delivery of the video that does not violate either constraint and results in a plan with the minimum peak bandwidth requirement, given the two constraints. The rate/time constrained bandwidth algorithm takes an additional parameter, *r*, the maximum allowable peak bandwidth requirement. Using *r*, *t*, and *b*, the rate/time constrained bandwidth smoothing algorithm allows the time constraint to be relaxed only when the rate constraint *r* would have otherwise been violated. A comparison with other bandwidth smoothing algorithms using both a Motion-JPEG encoded video and a MPEG encoded video are included.

In the next section, we briefly motivate the problems associated with delivering interactive video-on-demand in buffered environments. In Section 6.3, Section 6.4, and Section 6.5, we present the rate-constrained, time-constrained, and rate/time-constrained bandwidth smoothing algorithms, respectively. We then compare and contrast the various bandwidth smoothing algorithms in Section 6.6.

6.2 Delivering Video in Video-on-Demand Systems

For supporting the playback of stored video streams, it is commonly agreed that several levels of interactivity must be provided for in interactive video-on-demand systems [LITT94]. For our purposes, we expect there to be at least three levels of service: Strict Playback, Quasi-Interactive Playback, and Interactive Playback. To understand why, we will discuss the necessary support for these three methods

Strict Playback

In the strict playback mode, the user is forced to watch the video from the beginning to end without any change in the consumption rate. Creating bandwidth plans using one of the unlimited buffer algorithms makes resource allocation within the VOD system the simplest due to the fewer number of interactions (and for the CBA algorithm, the monotonicity of bandwidth allocations). In addition, for limited client-side buffers, using one of the minimal peak bandwidth algorithms is attractive for reducing the amount of resources allocated for guaranteed service. As an example, the minimum changes bandwidth algorithm allows the server to allocate resources on the order of tens of minutes with approximately 10 megabytes of client-side buffer and 2 to 3 Mbps streams. Because the bandwidth plans are fixed, the server is free to schedule bandwidth as tightly as possible, using peaks in some plans to fill valleys in others.

Quasi-Interactive Playback

In the quasi-interactive playback mode, the user is allowed to have limited VCR interactions. In this mode, a method called the *VCR window* can be used to allow users limited access to their videos [FENG96]. This is based upon the observation that the common VCR functions rewind, examine, stop, and pause can be handled by the client-side buffer *without* requiring additional bandwidth from the network and server to service. The *VCR window* can be appended with additional *VCR buffering* in order to

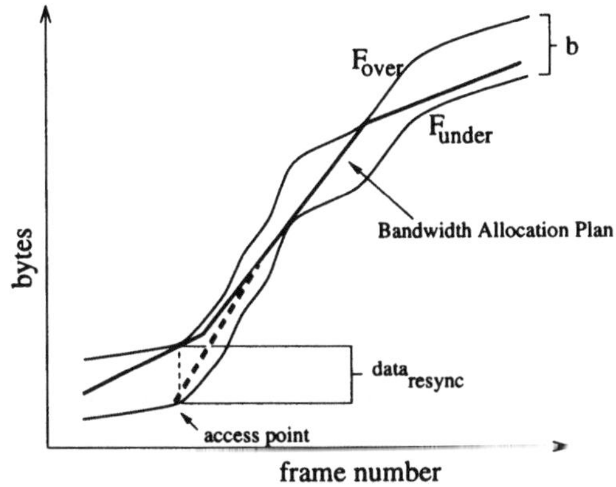

Figure 6.1: Supporting VCR Functionality. This figure shows the result of a scan to a random "access point" under bandwidth smoothing. With no overlap of data in the buffer, the distance between the bandwidth smoothing plan and F_{under} at the access point must be made up in order to continue along the original bandwidth plan. The dashed line shows a plan for resynchronizing to the original plan.

provide a larger VCR window for the user. Because the user can change its consumption rate, the streams cannot be scheduled as tightly as with in the strict playback case. However, in a system where the users abide by the *VCR window* the network and server resources can be allocated based on the peak bandwidth requirement *without* worrying about the user issuing a bandwidth request above and beyond what has been reserved.

Interactive Playback

Interactive playback for buffered, interactive VOD systems is perhaps the hardest resource allocation facing VOD designers. As an illustration, consider the bandwidth smoothing plan in Figure 6.1. When a random access is made from VCR functions such as a long fast-forward, excess channel capacity may have to be allocated in order to resynchronize the plan with the original peak bandwidth requirement. In this example, the server needs to send $data_{resync}$ bytes to make up the data that the client would have had during normal playback. In addition, enough resources need to be allocated to avoid buffer underflow. A sample plan for resynchronization is shown by the dotted line in Figure 6.1. As another illustration, consider a scan into an area that has a large number of large frame sizes. Under bandwidth smoothing these frames would have been prefetched in order to reduce the bandwidth requirement. However, a random access to these frames will require that (1) excess channel capacity be allocated, (2) reducing the quality of video until the plans are resynchronized, or (3) making the user wait until the buffer is filled. Due to the undeterministic nature of the interactions, providing guaranteed VCR interactivity can be difficult while maintaining a high network utilization. To aid in VCR functionality, ideas such as *contingency channels* can be useful [DAN94], where excess channel capacity is allocated for temporary allocation to VCR functionality. In the end, however, reducing the dependence on excess channel allocation will aid in the ability to provide interactive video-on-demand effectively. One such way to accomplish this is to reduce the buffer occupancy times (or the buffer utilization) for playback.

6.3 Rate-Constrained Bandwidth Smoothing

The critical bandwidth allocation (CBA) algorithm, minimum changes bandwidth allocation (MCBA) algorithm, and minimum variability bandwidth allocation (MVBA) algorithm (as described in Chapter 4) result in bandwidth smoothing plans that optimize the delivery of stored video under certain constraints. These algorithms all have the common property in that they have the smallest peak bandwidth requirements for a fixed-size client-side buffer. These algorithms, however, typically have large buffer occupancy requirements, resulting in smaller VCR-window sizes as well as larger contingency channel allocation requirements. To more tightly couple the client and server, and thereby minimize the buffer occupancy times, we introduce *rate-constrained bandwidth smoothing* (RCBS) for the delivery of stored video.

The RCBS algorithm results in plans for the delivery of stored video that have the smallest peak bandwidth requirements for a given buffer size as in the CBA, MCBA, and MVBA algorithms, but also maximizes the VCR-window size. To implement this algorithm, a maximum bandwidth rate r is specified. Using this peak rate constraint, each frame, i, in the movie is examined. The bandwidth requirements for the preceding frames leading up to frame i are then modified such that the bandwidth requirement for frame i is *no greater* than the peak bandwidth requirement. In the event that frame i is less than the rate constraint r, then no preceding frames are modified.

Formally, let r be the maximum rate constraint and *prefetch(i)* be the maximum frame j such that the average frame size from j to i is less than or equal to r. That is,

$$prefetch(i) = \left\{ \max \text{ j: } j \le i \text{ AND } \sum_{k=j}^{i} \frac{b_k}{(i-j+1)} < r \right\}$$

Thus, *prefetch(i)* is simply the first frame for which prefetching must be used in order to keep the bandwidth under the maximum rate constraint r. Similarly, let *bw(j,i)* be defined as

$$bw(j,i) = \begin{cases} 0 & \text{if prefetch(i)>j} \\ rem\left(\sum_{k=j}^{i} b_k, r\right) & \text{if prefetch(i)=j} \\ r & \text{if prefetch(i)<j} \end{cases}$$

This equation finds, given frames j and i, $j<i$, the bandwidth that would be needed on a frame j to keep the rate constraint until frame i. For the case where prefetch(i) equals j, bw(j,i) is the remainder from using rate r for frames $j+1$ to i. Using these

```
for (excess=0,i=n;  i>0  ;  i--)
   if (frame_size[i] > rate)
         /*** Build up buffering because ***/
         /*** rate constraint violated ***/
      excess += (frame_size[i]-rate);
      allocation[i] = rate;
   else
      if (excess > (rate - frame_size[i]))
         allocation[i] = rate;
         excess = excess - (rate - frame_size[i]);
      else
         allocation[i] = frame_size[i] + excess;
         excess = 0;
```

Figure 6.2: Rate-Constrained Bandwidth Smoothing Pseudo-code. This figure shows the pseudo-code for the PCBS algorithm. The variable *excess* holds the amount of data that needs to be prefetched in order to maintain the rate-constraint *rate*. The second *if* clause does the actual distribution of the prefetched data into previous frame slots.

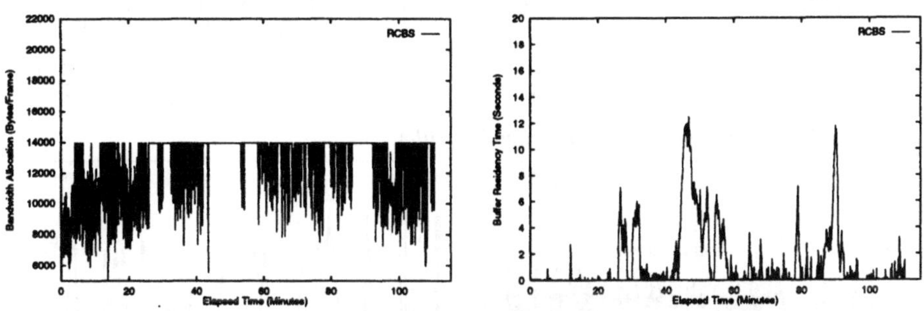

Figure 6.3: Rate Constrained Bandwidth Smoothing. This figure shows an example of the *rate-constrained bandwidth smoothing algorithm* for the Motion-JPEG compressed movie *Speed* using a 5 megabyte buffer. The right figure shows the buffer residency times for the same algorithm.

definitions, the bandwidth for any frame in the movie can then be written as:

$$c(i) = \max_{i \le k \le n} bw(i, k)$$

From an implementation standpoint, the RCBS plan can be calculated in O(n) by working from the end of the movie to the beginning and keeping track of the excess data that needs to be prefetched in order to maintain the rate constraint. The pseudo-code for this algorithm can be found in Figure 6.2. As shown by Figure 6.3, the RCBS algorithm has only modified a few regions within the movie. In particular, the largest rate-constrained region occurs around the 47 minute area within the movie. To highlight the difference between the RCBS algorithm and other bandwidth smoothing algorithms, we have also graphed sample bandwidth allocation plans for the CBA, MCBA, and MVBA algorithms (along with their buffer residency

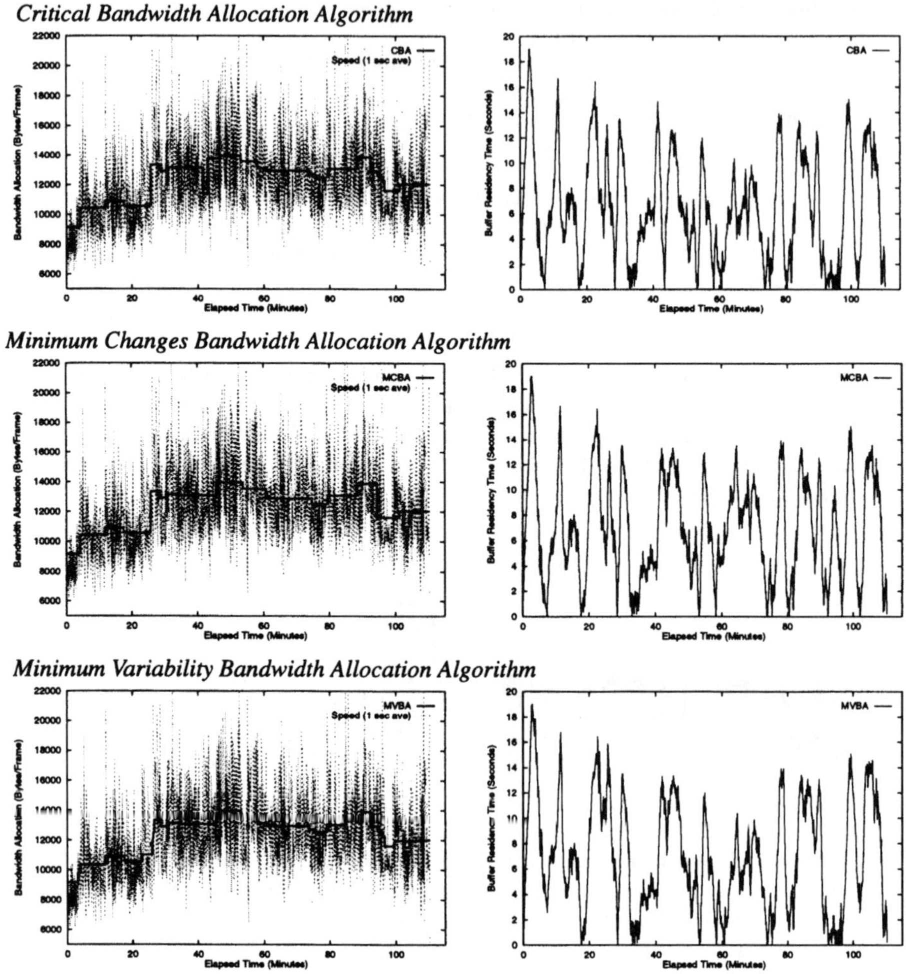

Figure 6.4: Bandwidth Smoothing Plans. This figure shows example bandwidth smoothing plans for the *critical bandwidth allocation algorithm,* the *minimum changes algorithm,* and the *minimum variability bandwidth smoothing algorithms* for the Motion-JPEG compressed movie *Speed* using a 5 megabyte buffer. The right figures show the buffer residency times that these algorithms use to achieve their smoothing.

requirements) in Figure 6.3.

Using the RCBS algorithm results in several key properties. First, given a maximum rate constraint *r*, the RCBS uses the minimum size buffer. That is, no other plan that delivers all the video data can use less buffer while retaining the same rate constraint *r*. Second, because the algorithm prefetches only when the rate constraint will be violated, it results in the tightest coupling between the client and server plans. This results in resynchronization times that are the smallest given the maximum rate constraint *r*.

Finally, while the RCBS algorithm takes as input a rate constraint *r*, we note that it is also possible for the RCBS algorithm to create plans given a fixed client-side buffer. To accomplish this, a binary search can be used to find the minimum rate-constraint that can be used. Because the RCBS algorithm is an O(n) algorithm, finding the appropriate rate constraint using a buffer size is roughly O(*n*log*r*). As shown in Figure 6.3(b), the buffer residency times are much smaller than in those found in Figure 6.3, particularly in regions where the rate constraint is not violated (ex. time 0-10 minutes).

6.4 Time Constrained Bandwidth Smoothing

For the delivery of video in interactive VOD systems, we would like to have the properties that the MCBA, MVBA, and CBA smoothing algorithms offer, but we would also like to set a maximum buffer residency time in order to limit the resychronization data required as in the RCBS algorithm. Creating a bandwidth plan using the RCBS algorithm allows for the delivery of stored video that minimizes the buffer residency times, but have significantly more fluctuations in bandwidth that are required. For interactive video-on-demand systems, some delay may be acceptable to the user, allowing some of the burstiness to be removed. In this section, we propose a *time constrained bandwidth smoothing* algorithm that limits the buffer residency times to a user defined limit of *t* frames.

For the time-constrained bandwidth smoothing algorithm (TCBA), we use the function $F_{under}()$ as the same function as discussed in Chapters 3 and 4, namely

$$F_{under}(k) = \sum_{i=0}^{k} f_i$$

where f_i is the size of frame i. For the $F_{over}()$ curve, however, we use the following function to determine each point on the $F_{over}()$ curve:

$$F_{over}(j) = min\{F_{under}(j) + b, F_{under}(j+t)\} \qquad (1 \le j \le N)$$

where b is the buffer size in bytes, t is the time constraint in number of frames, and N is the number of frames in the video. Note, we assume that:

$$F_{under}(k) = F_{under}(N) \qquad (k > N)$$

where N is the number of frames in the movie. The pseudo-code for the time-constrained bandwidth smoothing algorithm is shown in Figure 6.5

To graphically understand this procedure, Figure 6.6 shows the creation of a time-constrained bandwidth smoothing plan using the F_{under} and F_{over} curves. To create the bandwidth plan, each frame i is examined and the point $F_{over}()$ is calculated for that

```
max_del = maximum time constraint (in frames)
buff_size = client buffer size in bytes;

for (i=0; i<N ;i ++)
    Funder(i) = summation frames 0 to i

for (i=0; i<N ; i++)
    if (Funder[i]+buff_size < Funder[i+max_del])
        Fover[i] = Funder[i]+buff_size;
    else
        Fover[i] = Funder[i+max_del];

run bandwidth smoothing algorithm using Funder and Fover
    to get bandwidth plan.
```

Figure 6.5: Time-constrained bandwidth smoothing pseudo-code. This figure shows the pseudo-code for the algorithm. Details of the implementation and optimizations have been omitted.

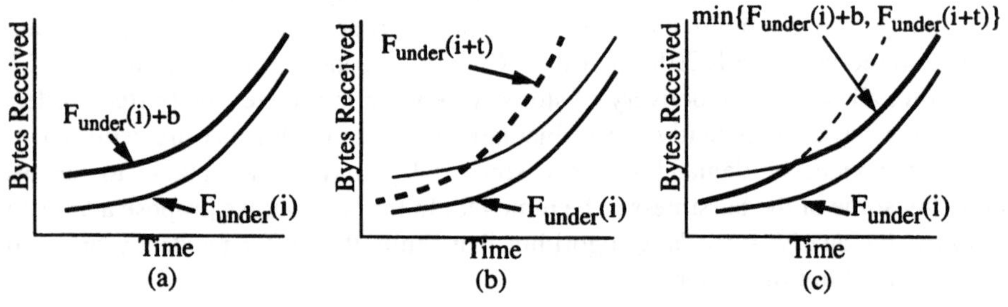

Figure 6.6: Time Constrained Bandwidth Smoothing. This figure shows how the function $F_{over}()$ is calculated for the time-constrained bandwidth smoothing algorithm for a buffer of size *b* bytes and a maximum time constraint of *t* frames. Figure (a) shows the curves that are used in the traditional bandwidth smoothing algorithms. Figure (b) shows the curve that is required to maintain the time constraint *t* frames. Figure (c) show the final function $F_{over}()$ that is used for the calculation of the bandwidth plan (heavy solid line). The adjustment of $F_{over}()$ guarantees that the prefetch buffer at frame *i* does not prefetch too much to violate the time constraint.

point. The figures (a) and (b) show the buffer requirement and time requirement calculations, respectively. As shown in Figure 6.6(c), the new $F_{over}()$ results in areas determined by the time constraint *t* as well as the buffer constraint *b*. In particular, in regions of very small frame sizes, as in the left side of Figure 6.6(c), $F_{over}()$ is determined by the time constraint *t*. In regions of large frames, $F_{over}()$ is determined by the buffer constraint *b*.

Once the curve $F_{over}()$ has been determined, *any* of the river-traversing bandwidth techniques can be applied to generate the bandwidth allocation plan used for play-

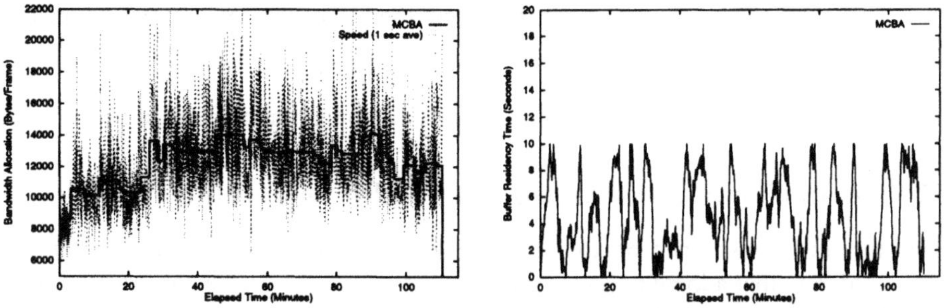

Figure 6.7: Time Constrained Bandwidth Smoothing Example. The left figure shows the *time-constrained* version for the *critical bandwidth allocation* algorithm for the movie *Speed* using a 5 megabyte buffer and a time constraint of 10 seconds. The right figure shows the buffer residency times for the same algorithm. Note how the buffer residency times were modified over those in Figure 6.3 and 6.4.

back. As an example, the *minimum changes bandwidth smoothing* algorithm can be used to generate the bandwidth plan with the new $F_{under}()$ and $F_{over}()$ curves. For a maximum time constraint *t* and a maximum buffer size *b*, the resulting plan then has the smallest peak bandwidth requirement and the smallest number of changes in bandwidth that meets *both* the time constraint and buffer constraint. Similarly, the *minimum variability bandwidth smoothing* algorithm may be used to create a plan that has the minimum peak bandwidth requirement and smallest variability of bandwidth requests for plans that meet the time and buffer constraints. A sample time-constrained bandwidth plan is shown in Figure 6.7, for the *minimum increases bandwidth algorithm*, a 5 megabyte smoothing buffer, and a time constraint of 300 frames. Compared with the bandwidth smoothing algorithm shown in Figure 6.3 and Figure 6.3, the time-constrained bandwidth smoothing algorithm results in an increase in the peak bandwidth requirement from 13968 bytes/frame to 14186 bytes/frame. Thus, the time-constrained bandwidth smoothing algorithm may result higher peak bandwidth requirements. The time-constrained bandwidth plans, however, adhere to a maximum buffer residency time.

At this point, several interesting points are worth discussing. Without the buffer time constraint *t*, it is still possible to enforce the buffer time constraint by adjusting the size of the buffer *b*, resulting in a $F_{over}()$ curve as with the traditional bandwidth smoothing techniques. However, this results in a time constraint that is determined by a few regions within the movie. Second, the time-constraint does not only apply to the segment at the peak bandwidth requirement. As shown by the buffer residency figures in Figure 6.3, the largest buffer residency requirements can occur at times where the bandwidth requirement is actually at its minimum (E.g. 0 to 10 minutes). As a result, using the time-constraint can minimize the prefetched data during non-peak bandwidth requirement segments as well. Third, the time constraint *t* does not necessarily imply that the user will have to wait *t* time units for every VCR function. The time constraint, rather, is a worst case delay when the network and server cannot allocate any additional resources to the client and where the buffer residency times happen to be at the maximum time constraint *t*. Finally, very large values of *t* will result in plans that are determined completely by the buffer constraint *b*, while very small values of *t* will result in a buffer that never fills completely due to the timing constraint.

6.5 Rate and Time Constrained Bandwidth Smoothing

Using the time-constrained bandwidth smoothing algorithm results in plans for the delivery of data that adhere to both a buffer constraint *b* and a time constraint *t*. For a given buffer size *b* and the time-constraint *t*, an increase in the peak bandwidth requirement may be required for continuous delivery over a plan determined by only the buffer size *b*. For smaller buffer sizes, as in our examples, the increase in the peak bandwidth requirement may not be that large. In other cases, however, a larger peak bandwidth requirement may be required, depending on the value of *t*. As a result, the user may want the bandwidth smoothing algorithm to both minimize the peak bandwidth requirement as well as adhere to the time-constraint *during non-peak bandwidth* segments. That is, the time-constraint is relaxed only during the peak bandwidth allocation segments.

Given a buffer size *b*, a time-constraint *t*, and a rate-constraint *r*, the *rate/time constrained bandwidth smoothing* (RTCBA) algorithm first adheres to the rate-constraint *r*, assuming that the rate-constraint is achievable with the given size buffer *b*. It accomplishes this by first using the RCBS algorithm to rate-constrain the frames in the movie. It then applies the time-constrained algorithm to the resultant plan. Two methods can be used to determine the rate-constraint *r*. First, the minimum rate *r* can be determined by running one of the river-charting bandwidth smoothing algorithms such as the CBA, MCBA, or MVBA algorithms using the buffer constraint *b*. Second, the rate constraint can be based on other factors such as the cost for peak bandwidth. To check whether or not the rate constraint is feasible with the buffer size *b*, the RCBS algorithm can be run to verify if the rate is possible.

To create the rate/time constrained bandwidth smoothing algorithm, a bandwidth plan is created using the O(n) RCBS algorithm that adheres to the rate-constraint *r*. The resulting plan is then examined to find regions in which the time-constraint *t* is violated. Note, the time constraint can only be violated in regions that use the peak bandwidth requirement *r*. If the time-constraint is violated, the section of the video is then marked as *untouchable*. Finally, the time-constrained bandwidth smoothing algorithm is run on the segments that are not marked *untouchable*. The pseudo-code for the algorithm is shown in Figure 6.8. A sample rate constrained bandwidth smoothing plan is shown in Figure 6.9. In this example, the regions around 43 minutes and 90 minutes are allowed to violate the time constraint of 10 seconds in order to minimize the peak bandwidth requirement for the 5 megabyte smoothing buffer.

```
max_del = maximum time constraint (in frames)
buff_size = client buffer size in bytes;

for (i=0; i<N ;i ++)
    F_under(i) = summation frames 0 to i

for (i=0; i<N ; i++)
    if (F_under[i]+buff_size < F_under[i+max_del])
        F_over[i] = F_under[i]+buff_size;
    else
        F_over[i] = F_under[i+max_del];

Determine minimum peak bandwidth req. based on buffer size b
Calculate Rate-constrained bandwidth plan at minimum peak bandwidth

For each region in the Rate-constrained bandwidth plan in
    which all frames do not violate the time constraint
    run bandwidth smoothing algorithm using F_under and F_over
            to get bandwidth plan for the region.
```

Figure 6.8: Rate/Time Constrained Smoothing Algorithm Pseudo-Code. Details of exact implementation have been omitted for brevity.

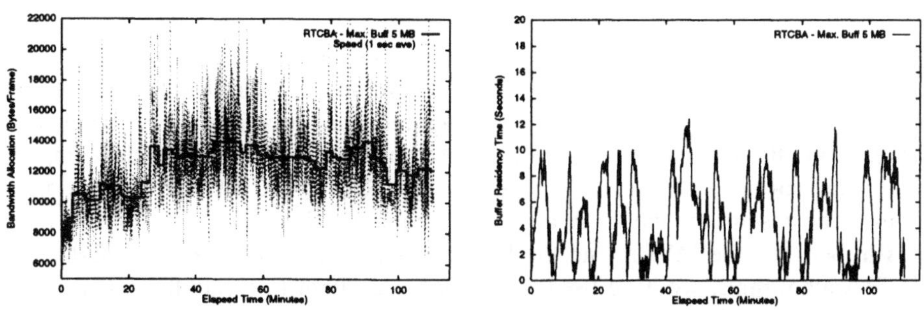

Figure 6.9: Rate/Time Constrained Bandwidth Smoothing Example. The left figure shows the *rate/time-constrained* version for the *critical bandwidth allocation* algorithm for the movie *Speed* using a 5 megabyte buffer and a time constraint of 10 seconds. The right figure shows the buffer residency times for the same algorithm. Note how the buffer residency times were modified over those in Figure 6.3.

6.6 Evaluation

To evaluate the time-constrained bandwidth smoothing algorithms, we selected the Motion-JPEG encoded movie *Speed* from the OSU video library suite and the MPEG encoded movie *Star Wars* available from Bellcore. We selected two different types of encodings to highlight the effect that the encoding has on the time-constrained algorithms. In particular, the Motion-JPEG compression standard has each frame compressed independently, resulting in a bit stream that does not take advantage of inter-frame redundancy. The MPEG video clip has three frame types that allow for greater compression ratios to be achieved. The important point here is that the time-constraint

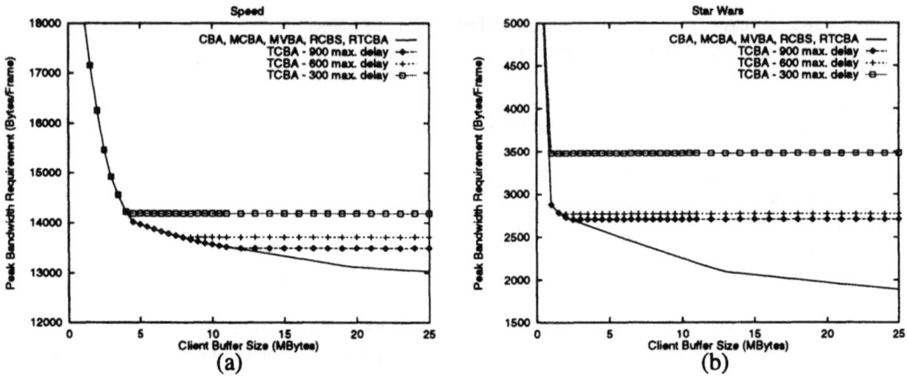

Figure 6.10: Peak Bandwidth Requirements. This figure shows the peak bandwidth requirements that are required for the various algorithms and the compressed video streams *Speed* and *Star Wars*.

is somewhat correlated to the bit-rate of the compressed video stream, assuming a fixed size buffer. For these video streams, the video *Speed* has an average bit rate of 3 megabits per second, while the video *Star Wars* has an average bit rate of approximately 500 kilobits per second.

For the delivery of the compressed video stream, several measures are important for the end-to-end resource guarantees. Among these are the peak bandwidth requirement, the number of bandwidth changes required, the variability of the bandwidth requests, and the average amount of data in the buffer (its utilization). In the comparison of the various algorithms, we have used the RCBS, MCBA, and MVBA algorithms. The results for the CBA algorithm (minimum increases algorithm) always falls in between the MVBA and the MCBA algorithm. Finally, for the TCBA and RTCBA algorithms, we have used the MCBA algorithm to create the actual bandwidth allocation plans once the time-constraint process has been run. Recall, the TCBA and RTCBA are multi-step algorithms that first determine F_{under} and F_{over} based on the time constraint and then use any of the river-charting bandwidth plans to create the actual bandwidth allocation plan.

6.6.1 Peak Bandwidth Requirements

For VOD systems that allocate resources based on the peak bandwidth requirements, minimizing the peak bandwidth requirement can increase the likelihood that the server and network have sufficient resources to handle the stream. In addition, a low peak rate may reduce the total cost of the data transfer. In Figure 6.10, we have graphed the peak bandwidth requirements for the movies *Speed* and *Star Wars* for the various bandwidth smoothing algorithms TCBA, RTCBA, MCBA, MVBA, and RCBS. As shown in Figure 6.10 (a), all algorithms except the TCBA algorithm have the same *minimum* peak bandwidth requirement given a fixed client-side buffer size. Given a time constraint *t* and the client side buffer size, the TCBA algorithm, results in plans that are buffer constrained for small buffer sizes and time constrained for larger buffer sizes, as expected. As an example, consider the time constraint $t=300$ frames. For the movie *Speed* and buffer sizes less than 4 megabytes, the buffer size limits the amount of data that can be prefetched, resulting in the same peak bandwidth requirements as using just the buffer size. Note, for buffer sizes less than 4 megabytes, there may be times when the time constraint is indeed violated, but it does not occur during the run(s) which force the minimum peak bandwidth requirement. For buffer sizes larger than 4 megabytes, the client-side buffer is large enough that the time constraint can be violated more often. Because the TCBA algorithm enforces this time constraint for all frames within the movie, the peak bandwidth curve is flat for all buffer sizes greater than 4 megabytes. By increasing the time constraint t, the point at which the TCBA algorithm switches from the buffer constraint to the time constraint also increase (although not linearly) as shown by the figure.

For the movie *Star Wars*, the TCBA algorithm has results in buffer constraint to time constraint cross-over points that are smaller than in the movie *Speed* (in terms of the buffer size). The main reason for this is that with smaller frame sizes, a given buffer size can, on average, hold more frames. This results in time constraints that are violated with smaller buffer sizes. Finally, we see in Figure 6.10 (b) that the asymptotic value for the 600 and 900 frame time constraints are much closer to each other than the 300 frame time constraint. Using the 300 frame time constraint does not allow much of the burstiness to be removed for the movie *Star Wars*. However, using the 600 frame time constraint allows nearly all the burstiness to be removed. Once the short term burstiness has been removed (as in the MPEG frame patterns), the time-constraint becomes more critical in the determination of the peak bandwidth requirement.

6.6.2 Number of Bandwidth Changes

Minimizing the number of bandwidth changes that a stream requires reduces the overhead involved with change the rate requirement for the stream. As an illustration, using a 5 megabyte buffer and the minimum changes bandwidth allocation algorithm for the delivery of the Motion-JPEG compressed video *Speed* results in a plan for the delivery of the video that has only 12 changes in bandwidth over the 2 hour duration of the movie. As a result, the network and server resources can be allocated approximately every 10 minutes before a change in bandwidth is required. Figure 6.11 shows the required bandwidth changes for the various bandwidth smoothing algorithms.

As shown in Figure 6.11 (a) and (d), we see the main drawback of the *rate-constrained bandwidth smoothing* (RCBS) algorithm. For the movie *Speed*, the RCBS algorithm requires more than 3 orders of magnitude more bandwidth changes than the other river-charting bandwidth plans. For the movie *Star Wars*, the RCBS algorithm requires nearly 4 orders of magnitude more bandwidth changes. In general, the RCBS algorithm requires a bandwidth change per frame for approximately 75% of the frames within the movie for small buffer sizes. In comparing the RCBS algorithm for

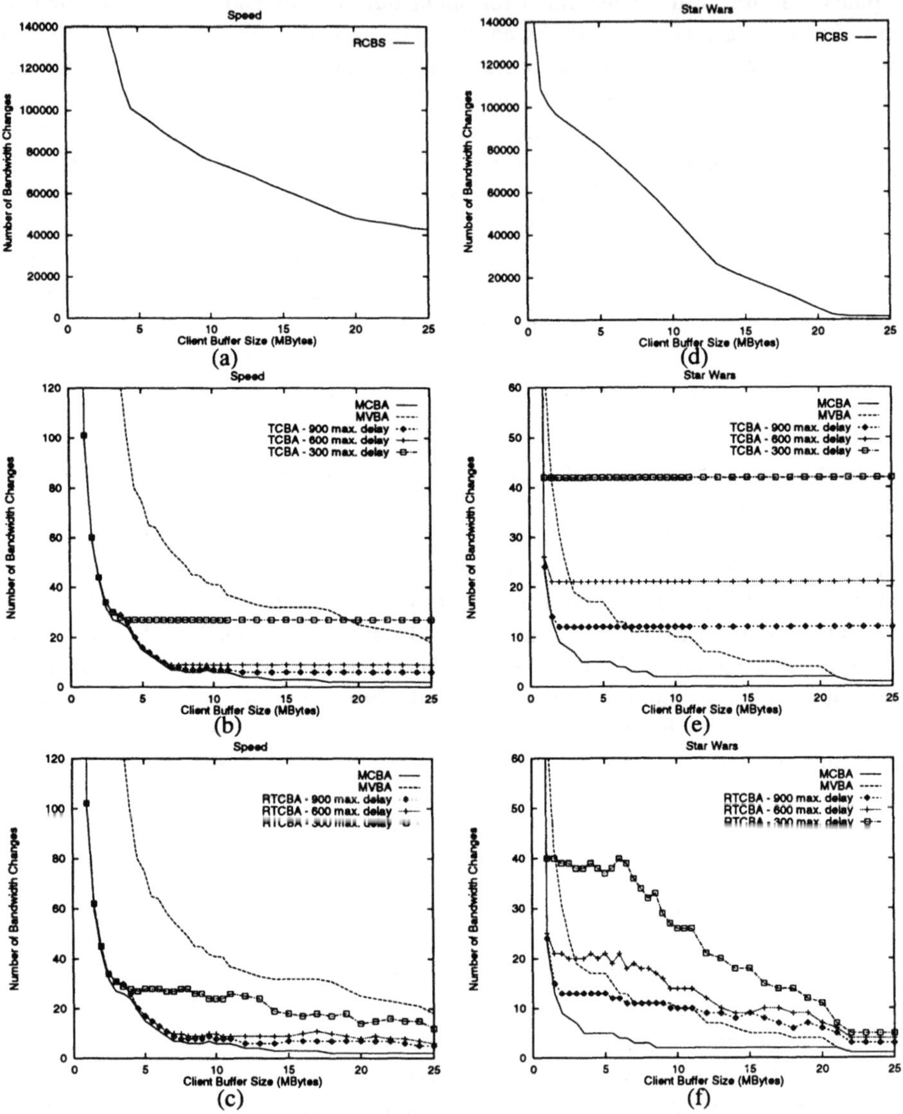

Figure 6.11: Number of Bandwidth Changes. This figure shows the number of bandwidth changes that the various algorithms require for the compressed video streams *Speed* and *Star Wars*.

the two movies, we see that the movie *Star Wars* has a lower asymptotic value than the movie *Speed.* The main reason for this is that much of the burstiness (due to the frame patterns in MPEG) are removed with small buffers. In addition, because the frames in *Star Wars* are smaller on average, the large buffer sizes can smooth much more of the data.

The number of changes required by the TCBA algorithm (using the minimum changes bandwidth allocation algorithm to create the bandwidth plan) are shown in Figure 6.11 (b) and (e). In Figure 6.11 (b), we see that the TCBA algorithm results in a graph that is similar to its peak bandwidth requirement graph. That is, for smaller buffer sizes, the graph is determined primarily by the buffer constraint, while for larger buffer sizes, the graph is determined primarily by the time constraint. Figure (b) also shows the main advantage of using the TCBA algorithm over the RCBS algorithm; it results in a total number of bandwidth changes that is at least the same order of magnitude as the MCBA algorithm.

The number of changes required by the RTCBA algorithm (using the minimum changes bandwidth allocation algorithm to create the bandwidth plan) are shown in Figure 6.11 (c) and (f). Here, we see that the RTCBA algorithm has fewer bandwidth changes than the TCBA algorithm, mainly due to the time-constraint being relaxed to meet the minimum peak bandwidth requirements. Figure 6.11 (f) shows that the RTCBA algorithm reduces the number of bandwidth changes at a quicker rate for the movie *Star Wars* than for the movie *Speed* (E.g. time constraint 900 in figure (f)). This is again due to the smaller frame sizes in the *Star Wars* video, resulting in larger regions that are at the minimum peak bandwidth requirement than in the movie *Speed* for a given buffer size.

6.6.3 Bandwidth Variation

In Figure 6.12, we have graphed the bandwidth variability exhibited by the various smoothing algorithms for the movies *Speed* and *Star Wars.* The bandwidth variability is the standard deviation of the rate requests on a per frame basis. As shown in Figure 6.12, we see that another advantage of using the TCBA algorithm over the RCBS algorithm is that the time-constrained algorithms result in similar bandwidth variability as the minimum variability bandwidth algorithm (MVBA). For the TCBA algorithm, the asymptotic values are horizontal as in the other performance metrics. Again, this is due to the fact that once the time-constraint is reached, adding more buffer does not change the bandwidth plan, resulting in the same variability.

6.6.4 Buffer Utilization

The RCBS algorithm was introduced to minimize the buffer residency requirements for the delivery of stored video. As a result, it is not particularly well suited for reducing the total number of rate changes or reducing the variability of bandwidth requirement of the network. In Figure 6.13, we have graphed the buffer utilizations for the various bandwidth smoothing algorithms. Here we see that the bandwidth smoothing algorithms that minimized the variability or minimized the number of bandwidth changes have the largest buffer utilization measurements (typically around 50%). In addition, we see that the RCBS algorithm has the smallest buffer utilization measurements, as expected. The TCBA algorithm has buffer utilizations that approach 0 for large buffer sizes, however, this is due to the fact that it has much higher peak band-

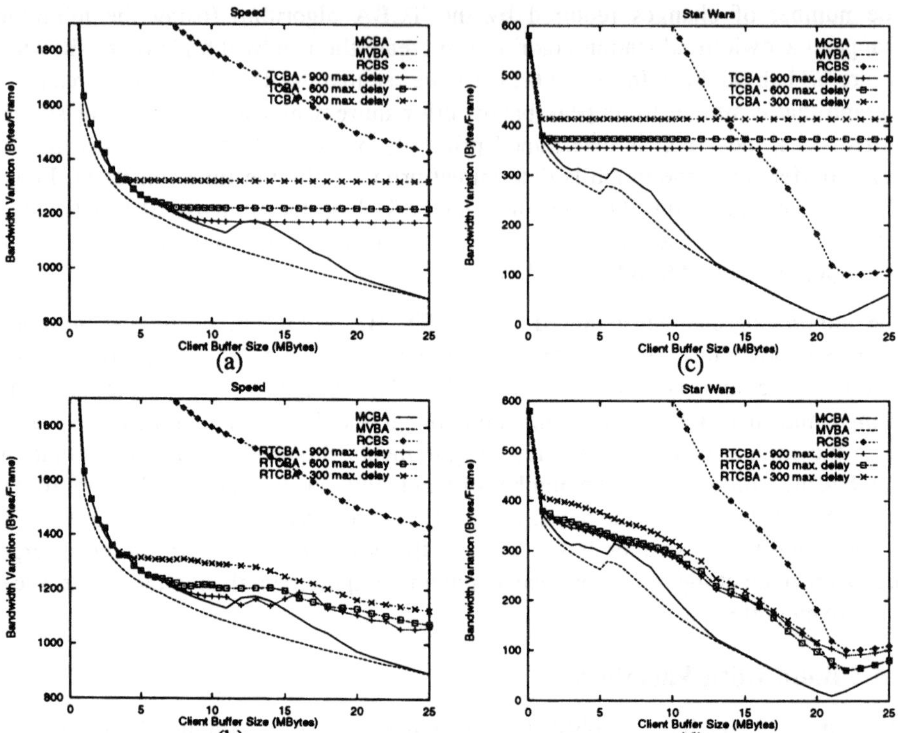

Figure 6.12: Bandwidth Variation. This figure shows the variation in bandwidth that each of the various algorithms require for the compressed video streams *Speed* and *Star Wars*.

width requirements in these areas. By using the RTCBA algorithm (and hence the same minimum peak bandwidth requirement), we see that the time-constrained bandwidth smoothing algorithms are in between the RCBS algorithm and the MCBA and MVBA algorithms. In particular, consider the graph shown in Figure 6.13 (d), we see that for buffer sizes in the range of 4-10 megabytes that the buffer utilizations of the RTCBA algorithms approach that of the RCBS algorithm, while still achieving similar number of bandwidth changes of the MCBA bandwidth smoothing algorithm. In general, as the time constraint is decreased for the RTCBA algorithm, the bandwidth plan used will continue to approach the RCBS algorithm. Finally, using large time constraints for the RTCBA algorithm, the bandwidth plan used will approach the minimum changes or minimum variability algorithms.

6.7 Summary

In this chapter, we have examined bandwidth smoothing techniques for the delivery of compressed prerecorded video streams. The MCBA, MVBA, and CBA algorithms

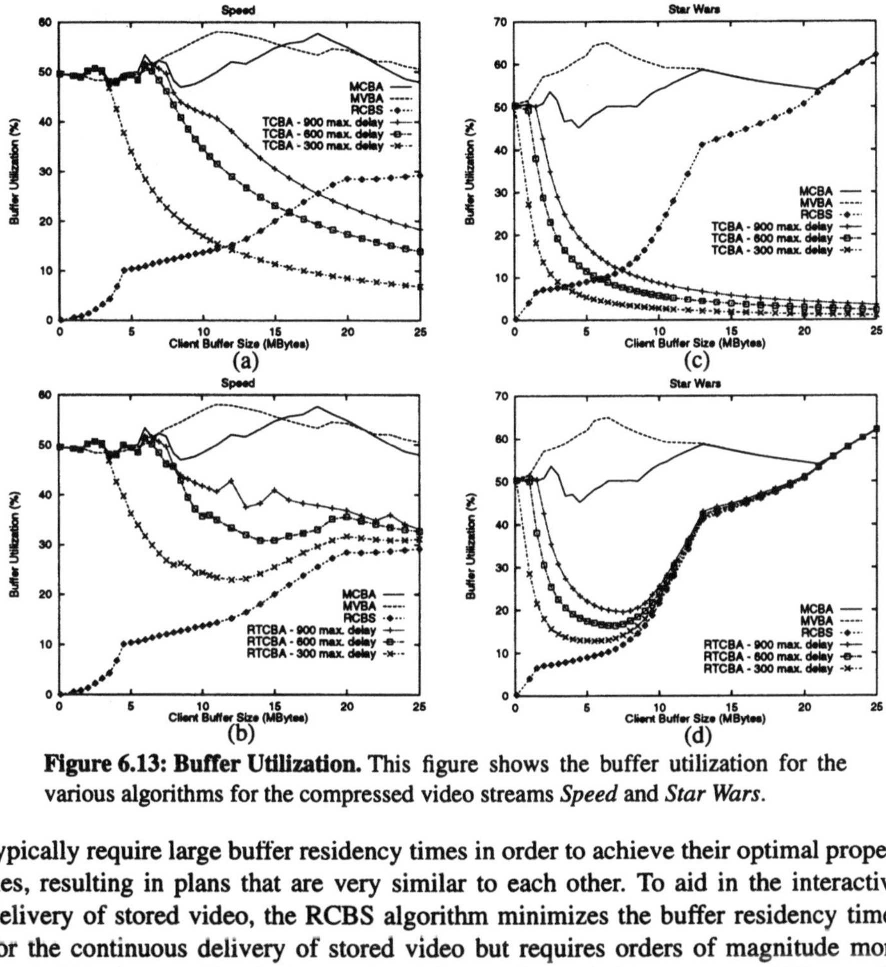

Figure 6.13: Buffer Utilization. This figure shows the buffer utilization for the various algorithms for the compressed video streams *Speed* and *Star Wars*.

typically require large buffer residency times in order to achieve their optimal properties, resulting in plans that are very similar to each other. To aid in the interactive delivery of stored video, the RCBS algorithm minimizes the buffer residency times for the continuous delivery of stored video but requires orders of magnitude more bandwidth changes. For the interactive delivery of stored video, we would like to take advantage of the properties that the MCBA, MVBA, and CBA algorithms have to offer, and we would also like to minimize the buffer residency times as well in order to aid in providing interactive service.

We have introduced the notion of *time-constrained* bandwidth smoothing. The *time-constrained bandwidth smoothing* algorithm allows the user to specify a maximum time constraint *t*, for which a frame can sit within the client-side buffer during continuous playback. By adjusting the calculation of the bandwidth plans, any of the well-known bandwidth smoothing techniques can be used to create plans that adhere to time and buffer requirement. For smaller values of *t*, the peak bandwidth requirement is typically defined by a single region within the video. To allow for more flexibility, we have introduced a rate/time constrained bandwidth smoothing algorithm that, given a fixed size client buffer, determines a plan that has the minimal peak bandwidth requirement and then adheres to the time constraint *t*. This algorithm then results in areas that may violate the time constraint which are allocated at the maximum rate constraint *r*. By using the time constraint *t*, a bandwidth plan can be created that takes advantage of the properties that the RCBS, MCBA, MVBA, and CBA algorithms have to offer, namely, reducing the number of rate changes while keeping the buffer residency times small.

7

CONCLUSIONS AND FUTURE DIRECTIONS

7.1 Conclusions

In this monograph, we have focused on the problem of transmitting stored variable-bit-rate video. Because the information about a stored video stream is known *a priori* to the start of playback, network and server resource requirements can be anticipated before any of the video data is actually transmitted. In addition, by using this information along with a client-side buffer, the resource requirements can be *smoothed* by prefetching large bursts of video data before they occur.

We have introduced the notion of *critical bandwidth allocation* (CBA) for the delivery of compressed prerecorded video. The CBA algorithm produces bandwidth plans that are monotonically decreasing. For systems where retrievals all follow these monotonically decreasing bandwidth plans, admission control is made simpler. That is, the network manager need only ask - *Is there enough bandwidth to start the flow of data*? For limited buffer sizes, the CBA algorithm produces plans for the continuous playback of video that have (1) the fewest number of bandwidth increases, (2) the smallest peak bandwidth requirements, and (3) the largest minimum bandwidth requirements. We have extended the critical bandwidth allocation technique and have introduced an *optimal bandwidth allocation* (OBA) technique. The optimal bandwidth allocation algorithm, in addition to the three properties of the CBA algorithm, also minimizes the number of bandwidth changes required for the continuous playback of video. As a result, the OBA plans require very few changes in bandwidth for relatively small amounts of buffering.

The use of smoothing for the delivery of stored video, implies that the plan may be inflexible to change. We have introduced the *VCR-window* technique which allows for full-function VCR capabilities within a small locality without requiring a change in the bandwidth reservations that were made. In the event that access is required outside of the VCR-window, a renegotiation of network bandwidth will be required. We have shown how contingency channels can be used for accesses outside of the VCR-window. Because contingency channels cannot always be guaranteed, the VCR-window is useful in minimizing the number of occurrences when the contingency channel will be used.

Finally, we have explored the notion of *rate-constrained bandwidth smoothing* and *time-constrained bandwidth smoothing*, each attempting to minimize the resource requirements for interactive video-on-demand systems. The *rate-constrained bandwidth smoothing algorithm* (RCBS) minimizes the buffer utilization as well as the buffer requirement for stored video by prefetching data only when the pre-defined rate constraint would otherwise be violated. The bandwidth plans that result, however, typically have many more rate changes than the CBA or OBA algorithms. To address this short-coming, we have introduced the notion of *time-constrained bandwidth smoothing* which attempts to bridge the gap between the CBA and OBA algorithms and the RCBS algorithm. The time-constrained algorithm accomplishes this by setting a maximum allowable prefetch time for each frame, allowing the number of rate changes to be greatly reduced while also being sensitive to the buffer utilization for interactive video delivery.

7.2 Future Directions

In this monograph, we have presented techniques for buffering variable-bit-rate video. Several interesting problems arise from the use of bandwidth smoothing techniques that we have not addressed here. We will briefly discuss these problems in this section and possible approaches that may be used.

First, the bandwidth smoothing techniques presented in Chapters 3 and 4 assume a maximum fixed-size buffer exists. For the delivery of compressed video to a set-top-box, this assumption may work well. For workstation environments, however, the availability of buffering in the client may dynamically change over time. As a result, a user may want the bandwidth smoothing to dynamically alter its prefetching based on the amount of available buffering. Like VCR interactivity, however, these dynamically generated plans can complicate the resource requirements that are already allocated.

Second, the bandwidth smoothing techniques presented assume that all the video data is delivered. In order to further aid the video-on-demand server, a user may be willing to accept a small amount of packet or frame loss in exchange for a reduced delivery charge. The question then arises - *Can bandwidth smoothing algorithms be used in conjunction with adaptive picture quality techniques to further reduce the resource requirements for the delivery of stored video?* In particular, modifying the picture quality can occur in two dimensions: temporally and spatially. In frames with high amounts of detail, a coarser quantization scale can be used to reduce the bit rate of the frames. Alternatively, during bursts of large frame sizes, the frame rate may be reduced to a slightly smaller level to reduce the average bit rate of the video stream. Because the bandwidth smoothing techniques work by prefetching frames of data well in advance determining *when* and *which* frames to alter is left as a new research area. By combining the techniques of bandwidth smoothing and adaptive quality techniques, it appears that the streams can be made even less bursty then just using adaptive quality techniques.

Third, there are a set of applications that fall in between live and stored video. We refer to these applications as *delayed* video. Delayed video is a broadcast video that is not necessarily stored, such as a newscast or sports event. These applications do not have the short delay requirements of live-video, but also may not have the entire video *a priori* to broadcast. As a result, hybrid bandwidth smoothing techniques that do not have all the video data available are required. It is clear that for very small delays, the techniques used will be similar to those developed for live video, and that for very large delays, the techniques used will be similar to those developed for stored video. An introduction to this problem can be found in [REX97]

Finally, the VCR-window, contingency channels, and time-constrained bandwidth smoothing techniques are a step towards implementing a true interactive video-on-demand system, however, the interactivity aspect is still not completely understood. The size required for the VCR-window depends on the encoding of the video as well as the interactivity that users require. If most users have very minor adjustments to their bandwidth plans, then the VCR-window can filter many adjustments through buffering. The size requirement for the contingency channel is also dependent on the actual usage patterns in the video-on-demand system. These buffer requirements and contingency channel requirements probably will require an iterative refinement through implementation and experimentation.

REFERENCES

ANDE92 D. Anderson, Y. Osawa, R. Govindan, "A File System for Continuous Media", *ACM Transactions on Computer Systems*, Vol. 10, No. 4, Nov, 1992, pp. 311-337.

ARAS94 C.M. Aras, J.F. Kurose, D.S. Reeves, H. Schulzrinne, "Real-time Communication in Packet Switched Networks", *Proceedings of the IEEE*, Vol. 82, No. 1, pp. 122-139, Jan. 1994.

BANE94 A. Banerjea, E.W. Knightly, F.L. Templin, H. Zhang, "Experiments with the Tenet Real-Time Protocol Suite on the Sequoia 2000 Wide Area Network", In Proceedings of *ACM Multimedia 1994*, San Francisco, CA, Oct. 1994, pp. 183-191.

CCUB91 C-Cube Microsystems, "Designing JPEG Video Systems with the C-Cube CL550", C-Cube Microsystems, Milpitas, CA, 1991.

CCIT93 CCITT Recommendation MPEG-1, "Coded Representation of Picture, Audio, and Multimedia/ Hypermedia Information," ISO/IEC 11172, Geneve Switzerland, 1993.

CHEN94 M.S. Chen, D.D. Kandlur, P.S. Yu, "Support for Fully Interactive Playout in a Disk-Array-Based Video Server", In Proceedings of *ACM Multimedia 1994*, San Francisco, CA, Oct. 1994, pp. 391-398.

COHE94 D.M. Cohen, D.P. Heyman, "A Simulation Study of Video Teleconferencing Traffic in ATM Networks", In Proceedings of *IEEE INFOCOM 1993*, pp. 894-901.

DAN94 A. Dan, D. Sitaram, P. Shahabuddin, "Scheduling Policies for an On-Demand Video Server with Batching", In Proceedings of *ACM Multimedia 1994*, San Francisco, CA, Oct. 1994, pp. 15-23.

DAN94a A. Dan, P. Shahabuddin, D. Sitaram, D. Towsley, "Channel Allocation under Batching and VCR Control in Movie-On-Demand Servers", *IBM Research Report RC19588*, Yorktown Heights, NY, 1994.

DEGE95 M. Degermark, T. Kohler, S. Pink and O. Schelen, "Advance Reservations for Predictive Service", In Proceedings of *5th Intl. Workshop on Network and Operating System Support for Digital Audio and Video*, Durham, New Hampshire, April 18-21, 1995, pp. 3-14.

DEY94 J.K. Dey, C.S. Shih, M. Kumar, "Storage Subsystem in a Large Multimedia Server for High-Speed Network Environments," In Proceedings of *IS&T/SPIE Symposium on Electronic Imaging Science and Technology*, San Jose, CA, Feb. 1994.

DEYS94 J. Dey-Sircar, J. Salehi, J. Kurose, D. Towsley, "Providing VCR Capabilities in Large-Scale Video Servers", In Proceedings of *ACM Multimedia 1994*, San Francisco, CA, Oct. 1994, pp. 25-32.

FEDE94 C. Federighi, L. Rowe, "A Distributed Hierarchical Storage Manager for a Video-on-Demand System", In Proceedings of *1994 IS&T/SPIE Symposium on Electronic Imaging: Science and Technology*, San Jose, CA Feb. 1994.

FENG95 W. Feng, S. Sechrest, "Smoothing and Buffering for Delivery of Prerecorded Compressed Video", In Proceedings of *IS&T/SPIE Multimedia Computing and Networking*, Feb. 1995, San Jose, CA, pp. 234-242.

FENG95a W. Feng, S. Sechrest, "Critical Bandwidth Allocation for the Delivery of Compressed Prerecorded Video", *Computer Communications*, Vol. 18, No. 10, Oct. 1995, pp. 709-717.

FENG95b W. Feng, F. Jahanian, S. Sechrest, "An Optimal Bandwidth Allocation Strategy for the Delivery of Compressed Prerecorded Video", CSE-Technical Report 260-95, University of Michigan, Sept. 1995.

FENG97 W. Feng, F. Jahanian, S. Sechrest, "An Optimal Bandwidth Allocation Strategy for the Delivery of Compressed Prerecorded Video", *ACM/Springer-Verlag Multimedia Systems Journal,* 1997.

FENG97a W. Feng, "Rate-Constrained Bandwidth Smoothing for the Delivery of Stored Video", in *Proceedings of the 1997 SPIE Multimedia Computing and Networking Conference*, San Jose, CA, Feb. 1997.

FENG95c W. Feng, F. Jahanian, S. Sechrest, "A Network Cost Model for the Critical Bandwidth Allocation Approach," In Proceedings of *IASTD/ISMM International Conference on Distributed Multimedia Systems and Applications*, Stanford, CA, Aug. 1995.

FENG96 W. Feng, F. Jahanian, S. Sechrest, "Providing VCR Functionality in a Constant Quality Video-On-Demand Transportation Service", In Proceedings of *3rd IEEE International Conference on Multimedia Computing and Systems,* Hiroshima, Japan, June 1996.

FENG95d W. Feng, F. Jahanian, S. Sechrest, "Providing VCR Functionality in a Constant Quality Video-On-Demand Transportation Service", CSE-TechReport 271-95, Dec. 1995.

FENG96a W. Feng, S. Sechrest, "Improving Data Caching for Software MPEG Video Decompression", In *IS&T/SPIE Digital Video Compression: Algorithms and Technologies 1996*, San Jose, CA, Feb. 1996.

FENG96b W. Feng, "Video-On-Demand Services: Efficient Transportation and Decompression of Variable Bit Rate Video", Ph.D. Thesis, University of Michigan, April 1996.

FERR94 D. Ferrari, A. Banerjea, H. Zhang, "Network Support for Multimedia: A Discussion of the Tenet Approach", *Computer Networks and ISDN Systems*, Vol. 26, 1994, pp. 1267-1280

FERR95 D. Ferrari, A. Gupta and G. Ventre, "Distributed Advance Reservation of Real-Time Connections", In Proceedings of 5th Intl. Workshop on Network and Operating System Support for Digital Audio and Video, Durham, New Hampshire, April 18-21, 1995, pp. 15-26.

GEMM95 D.J. Gemmell, H.M. Vin, D. Kandlur, P.V. Rangan, L.A. Rowe, "Multimedia Storage Servers: A Tutorial", *IEEE Computer*, Vol. 28, No. 5, May 1995, pp. 40-49.

GEMM92 D.J. Gemmell, J.Han, "Principles of Delay Sensitive Multimedia Data Storage and Retrieval," *ACM Transactions on Information Systems*, Vol. 10, No. 1, Jan. 1992, pp. 51-90.

GHAN93 M. Ghanbari, V. Seferidis, "Cell-Loss Concealment in ATM Video Codecs", *IEEE Transactions on Circuits and Systems for Video Technology*, Vol. 3, No. 3, June 1993, pp. 238-247.

GONG95 K.L. Gong, L.A. Rowe, "Berkeley MPEG-1 User's Guide", University of California - Berkeley, Jan. 1995.

GOYA96 Pawan Goyal, Harrick M. Vin, "Network Algorithms and Protocol for Multimedia Servers", In Proceedings of *INFOCOM 1996,* San Francisco, CA, March 1996, pp. 1371-1379.

GROS95 M. Grossglauser, S. Keshav, and D. Tse, "RCBR: A Simple and Efficient Service for Multiple Time-Scale Traffic", in *Proceedings of ACM SIGCOMM*, pp. 219-230, Aug. 1995.

JEFF92 K. Jeffay, D.L. Stone, T. Talley, F.D. Smith, "Adaptive, Best-Effort, Delivery of Audio and Video Data Across Packet-Switched Networks", In Proceedings of *Third International Workshop on Network and Operating System Support for Digital Audio and Video*, La Jolla, CA, Nov. 1992, pp. 3-14.

KANA93 H. Kanakia, P.P. Mishra, A. Reibman, "An Adaptive Congestion Control Scheme for Real-Time Packet Video Transport", In *Proceedings of ACM SIGCOMM 1993*, September 1993, pp. 20-31.

KAND94 D. Kandlur, M. Chen, Z.Y. Shae, "Design of a Multimedia Storage Server" , In *IS&T/SPIE Symposium on Electronic Imaging Science and Technology,* San Jose, CA, Feb. 1994.

KATS94 H.P. Katseff, B.S. Robinson, "Predictive Prefetch in the Nemesis Multimedia Information Service", In Proceedings of *ACM Multimedia 1994,* San Francisco, CA, Oct. 1994, pp. 201-209.

LAM94 S. Lam, S. Chow, D. Yau, "An Algorithm for Lossless Smoothing of MPEG Video", In Proceedings of *ACM SIGCOMM 1994,* 1994.

LEGA91 D.J. LeGall, "A Video Compression Standard for Multimedia Applications," *Communications of the ACM,* Vol. 34, No. 4, (Apr. 1991), pp. 46-58.

LITT94 T.D.C. Little, D. Venkatesh, "Prospects for Interactive Video-On-Demand", *IEEE Multimedia,* Vol. 1, No. 3, Fall 1994, pp. 14-24.

LOUG93 P. Lougher, D. Shepherd, "The Design of a Storage Sever for Continuous Media", *The Computer Journal,* Vol. 36, No. 1, Feb. 1993, pp. 32-42.

MCMA96 J.M. McManus, K.W. Ross, "Video-On-Demand Over ATM: Constant-Rate Transmission and Transport", in *Proceedings of IEEE INFOCOM,* pp. 1357-1362, March 1996.

MCMA97 J.M. McManus, K.W. Ross, "A Dynamic Programming Methodology for Managing Prerecorded VBR Sources in Packet-Switched Networks", Unpublished report (Univ. of Pennsylvania), January 1997.

PANC94 P. Pancha, M. El Zarki, "MPEG Coding for Variable Bit-Rate Video Transmission", *IEEE Communications Magazine,* Vol. 32, No.5, May 1994, pp. 54-66.

PANC92 P. Pancha, M. El Zarki, "Prioritized Transmission of Variable Bit Rate MPEG Video", In *IEEE GLOBECOM 1992,* Dec. 1992, pp. 1135-1139.

PANC93 P. Pancha, M. El Zarki, "Bandwidth Allocation Schemes for Variable Bit Rate MPEG Sources in ATM Networks," *IEEE Transactions on Circuits and Systems for Video Technology,* Vol. 3, No. 3, June 1993, pp. 190-198.

PANC93a P. Pancha, M. El Zarki, "Bandwidth Requirements of Variable Bit Rate Sources in ATM Networks", In Proceedings of *INFOCOM 1993,* March 1993, pp. 902-909.

PARE92 A. Parekh, "A Generalized Processor Sharing Approach to Flow Control in Integrated Services Networks",Ph.D. Thesis, The Massachusetts Institute of Technology, 1992.

PATE93 K. Patel, B.C. Smith, L.A. Rowe, "Performance of a Software MPEG Video Decoder", In Proceedings of *ACM Multimedia 1993,* Anaheim, CA, August 1993, pp. 75-82.

RAMA93 S. Ramanathan, P. V. Rangan, "Adaptive Feedback Techniques for Synchronized Multimedia Retrieval over Integrated Networks," *IEEE/ACM Transactions on Networking,* Vol. 1, No. 2, April 1993, pp. 246-260.

RANG91 P. Venkat Rangan, H.M. Vin, "Designing File Systems for Digital Video and Audio", In *Proceedings of the 13th ACM Symposium on Operating Systems Principles,* Operating Systems Review, Vol. 25, No. 5, October 1991, pp. 81-94.

RANG93 P. Venkat Rangan, H.M. Vin, "Efficient Storage Techniques for Digital Continuous Multimedia," *IEEE Transactions on Knowledge and Data Engineering,* Vol. 5, No. 4, Aug. 1993, pp. 564-573.

REIN93 D. Reininger, D. Raychaudhuri, et. al, "Statistical Multiplexing of VBR MPEG Compressed Video on ATM Networks", In Proceedings of *IEEE INFOCOM 1993,* March 1993, pp. 919-926.

REX97 J. Rexford, S. Sen, J. Dey, W. Feng, J. Kurose, J. Stankovic, D. Towsley, "Online Smoothing of Live, Variable-Bit-Rate Video" , In Proceedings of *International Workshop on Network and Operating Systems Support for Digital Audio and Video (NOSSDAV '97),* May 1997.

ROWE94 L.A. Rowe, K. D. Patel, B.C. Smith, K. Liu, "MPEG Video in Software: Representation, Transmission, and Playback", In Proceedings of *High Speed Networking and Multimedia Computing, IS&T/SPIE Symposium on Electronic Imaging, Science, and Technology*, San Jose, CA Feb. 1994.

ROWE94a L. Rowe, "Video Compression, What to Do When Everything is Changing", *Invited Talk Usenix 1994.*

ROWE92 L.A. Rowe, B.C. Smith, "A Continuous Media Player", In Proceedings of the *3rd International Workshop on Network and Operating System Support for Digital Audio and Video*, San Diego, CA, Nov. 1992.

SALE96 J.D. Slaehi, Z.L. Zhang, J.F. Kurose, D. Towsley, "Optimal Buffering for the Delivery of Compressed Prerecorded Video", in *Proceedings of ACM SIGMETRICS*, pp. 222-231, May 1996.

SHEN95 P. J. Shenoy, H. M. Vin, "Efficient Support for Scan Operations in Video Servers", In Proceedings of the *3rd ACM Conference on Multimedia*, October, 1995.

STON93 D. Stone, K. Jeffay, "Queue Monitoring: A Delay Jitter Management Policy", In Proceedings of the *4th International Workshop on Network and OS Support for Digital Audio and Video*, 1993.

VIN94 H.M. Vin, P. Goyal, A. Goyal, A. Goyal, "A Statistical Admission Control Algorithm for Multimedia Servers", In Proceedings of *ACM Multimedia 1994*, San Francisco, CA, Oct. 1994, pp. 33-40.

VIN93 H.M. Vin, P.V. Rangan, "Designing a Multi-user HDTV Storage Server," *IEEE Journal on Selected Areas in Communications*, Vol. 11, No. 1, Jan. 1993, pp. 152-164.

WALL91 G.K. Wallace, "The JPEG Still Picture Compression Standard," *Communications of the ACM*, Vol. 34, No. 4, (Apr. 1991), pp. 30-44.

WILL93 P. Willis, "MPEG-2 Digital TV All Set to Go", *Electronics World and Wireless World*, Vol. 99, No. 5, May 1993, pp. 356-357.

WOLF95 L. Wolf, L. Delgrossi, R. Steinmetz, S. Schaller and H. Wittig, "Issues of Reserving Resources in Advance", In Proceedings of *5th Intl. Workshop on Network and Operating System Support for Digital Audio and Video*, Durham, New Hampshire, April 18-21, 1995, pp. 27-37.

ZHAN91 H. Zhang, S. Keshav, "Comparison of Rate-Based Service Disciplines", In Proceedings of *ACM SIGCOMM '91*, Sept. 1991, pp. 113-121.

INDEX

MIX
Papier aus verantwortungsvollen Quellen
Paper from responsible sources
FSC® C105338

If you have any concerns about our products,
you can contact us on
ProductSafety@springernature.com

In case Publisher is established outside the EU,
the EU authorized representative is:
Springer Nature Customer Service Center GmbH
Europaplatz 3, 69115 Heidelberg, Germany

Printed by Libri Plureos GmbH
in Hamburg, Germany